THEMATIC UNIT
MEDIEVAL TIMES

Written by Cynthia Ross

Illustrated by Cheryl Buhler

Teacher Created Materials, Inc.

6421 Industry Way

Westminster, CA 92683

www.teachercreated.com

©1992 Teacher Created Materials, Inc.

Reprinted, 2001

Made in U.S.A.

ISBN 1-55734-291-1

Table of Contents

Introduction **3**

Robin Hood of Sherwood Forest by Ann McGovern (Scholastic, 1968) **5**
(Available from Scholastic, CAN and UK; Ashton Scholastic, AUS)
    Summary—Sample Plan—Overview of Activities—Robin Hood's Hideout—Sequencing and Summary—Mathematics in Sherwood Forest

Adam of the Road by Elizabeth Jane Gray (Penguin, 1942, 1987) **14**
(Available from Penguin, CAN; Penguin LTD, UK and AUS)
    Summary—Sample Plan—Overview of Activities—Cinquains—Missing Animal Report— Crossword Puzzle—Discussion Questions—Medieval Daisy Chains

The Door in the Wall by Marguerite de Angeli (Dell, 1949, 1990) **24**
(Available from Bantam Doubleday Dell Corgi Seal, CAN; Bantam Doubleday Dell, UK; Transworld Publishing, AUS)
    Summary—Sample Plan—Overview of Activities—Coat of Arms—My Coat of Arms— Plaster Block Carvings—Word Shield Word Hunt—Discussion Questions

Poetry and Ballads **32**
The Singers of Ballads—Activities for Using Ballads—"Lord Randal"—"Barbara Allen"— Comprehension Questions—"Barbara Allen" and "Lord Randal" Comparison— "London Bridge"— Create a Ballad

Across the Curriculum **40**

Language Arts:	Questions for Writing and Discussion—Comprehension Techniques—Characters and their Characteristics—Journal Writing—Comparison Chart—Dear Diary
Math:	Medieval Math
Science:	The Art of Butchery—Very Berry Ink
Social Studies:	The Feudal System—Scribe, Take a Letter—Map Sizing—Grid for Map Graphing—Knights and Armor—Suit of Armor—A Knight in Armor—Castles on the Net—Off to the Crusades!
Art:	Tin Can Lanterns—Orange Pomander Ball—Mural or Banner
Music:	Minstrel's Flute
Life Skills:	Archery

Culminating Activities **66**
    A Medieval Festival—Recipes—Research Project

Unit Management **70**
Bulletin Board Ideas—Clip Art—Decorative Letters Scroll—Project Award and Invitation

Bibliography **77**
Answer Key **79**

Introduction

Medieval Times contains a captivating whole-language, thematic unit. Its pages are filled with a wide variety of lesson ideas and reproducible pages designed for use with intermediate and junior high school children. At its core are three high-quality, Newbery Award winning literature selections, *Adam of the Road, The Door in the Wall,* and *Robin Hood of Sherwood Forest.* They are high interest stories with excellent illustrations and varied reading levels. "Lord Randal" and "Barbara Allen" are well known ballads that are frequently alluded to in higher level literary readings.

There are activities included for each selection which set the stage for reading, encourage enjoyment of the book, and extend the concepts. In addition, the theme is connected to the curriculum with activities in language arts, daily writing assignments, math, science, social studies, art, music, and life skills. Many of these activities encourage cooperative learning. The majority of them were planned with the idea of interrelationship. Many overlap each story and can be used with any of the selections.

Challenging thematic units should be planned with an understanding of the reading and organizational abilities of the individuals and the unique group that will be participating in the unit. Some classes will take more time to cover the unit, while others will be able to do more projects independently or in cooperative learning groups.

One or all of the texts can be covered in a unit. They all depict life in the Middle Ages for an older child or pre-teen in about the 13th century. Adolescents seem to have trouble understanding that the world has not always been as it is now. Identifying the changes in civilization and the similarities or consistencies in human nature should be stressed.

The thematic unit includes:

❏ **literature selections**—summaries of three children's books with related lessons (complete with reproducible pages) that cross the curriculum

❏ **planning guides**—suggestions for sequencing lessons each day of the unit

❏ **poetry**—suggested selections and lessons enabling students to write their own works

❏ **writing ideas**—writing activities across the curriculum

❏ **bulletin board ideas**—suggestions and plans for student-created bulletin boards

❏ **curriculum connections**—in language arts, math, science, social studies, art, music, and life skills

❏ **group projects**—to foster cooperative learning

❏ **culminating activities**—which require students to synthesize their learning and produce products that can be shared with others

❏ **a bibliography**—suggesting additional literature and nonfiction books on the theme

---

To keep this valuable resource intact so that it can be used year after year, you may wish to punch holes in the pages and store them in a three-ring binder.

Introduction *(cont.)*

Why a Balanced Approach?

The strength of a whole-language approach is that it involves children in using all modes of communication—reading, writing, listening, illustrating, and doing. Communication skills are interconnected and integrated into lessons that emphasize the whole of language. Balancing this approach is our knowledge that every whole—including individual words—is composed of parts, and directed study of those parts can help a student to master the whole. Experience and research tell us that regular attention to phonics, other word attack skills, spelling, etc., develops reading mastery, thereby fulfilling the unity of the whole language experience. The child is thus led to read, write, spell, speak, and listen confidently in response to a literature experience introduced by the teacher. In these ways, language skills grow rapidly, stimulated by direct practice, involvement, and interest in the topic at hand.

Why Thematic Planning?

One very useful tool for implementing a balanced language program is thematic planning. By choosing a theme with correlating literature selections for a unit of study, a teacher can plan activities throughout the day that lead to a cohesive, in-depth study of the topic. Students will be practicing and applying their skills in meaningful contexts. Consequently, they will tend to learn and retain more. Both teachers and students will be freed from a day that is broken into unrelated segments of isolated drill and practice.

Why Cooperative Learning?

Besides academic skills and content, students need to learn social skills. This area of development cannot be taken for granted. Students must learn to work cooperatively in groups in order to function well in modern society. Group activities should be a regular part of school life, and teachers should consciously include social objectives as well as academic objectives in their planning. For example, a group working together to solve a problem may need to select a leader. Teachers should make clear to the students the qualities of good leader-follower group interaction just as they would state and monitor the academic goals of the project.

Why Internet Extenders?

Internet extenders have been added to many of the activities in this book to enhance them through quality Web sites. This supplemental information helps to expand the students' knowledge of the topic, as well as make them aware of the many valuable resources to be found on the Internet. Some Web sites lend themselves to group research; other sites are best viewed by the entire class. If one is available, use a large-screen monitor when the entire class is viewing the Web site and discussing its content.

Although these Web sites have been carefully selected, they may not exist forever. Teacher Created Materials attempts to offset the ongoing problem of sites which move, "go dark," or otherwise leave the Internet after a book has been printed. If you attempt to contact a Web site listed in this unit and find that it no longer exists, check the TCM home page at www.teachercreated.com for updated URL's for this book.

Robin Hood of Sherwood Forest

by Ann McGovern

Summary

Robin Hood is a folk tale in the form of an adventure romance. It began as a ballad in the Middle Ages.

Robin Hood was the rightful Earl of Huntington, but because the times were so corrupt, his family lost their lands and Robin was driven into the forest. The story demonstrates his method of protest, organizing a band of outlaws in Sherwood Forest and robbing the rich to support the poor until King Richard could return from the Crusades and right the wrongs committed by the tyrant Prince John. The adventure tells of Robin Hood's courage, skill at archery, and daring deeds in support of the poor.

This outline is a suggested plan for using the various activities that are presented in this book. You should adapt these ideas to fit your own classroom situation and the ability level of your students.

Sample Plan

Lesson 1

• Introduce the Middle Ages (from 1066 to 1400 A.D.).

• Introduce historical characters (page 6).

• Use *Illuminations* by Jonathan Hunt and discuss vocabulary and pictures.

• View a movie and listen to music from the Middle Ages (page 6).

Lesson 2

• Explore a map of England.

• Do Map Sizing activity (pages 53-54).

• Complete Comparison Chart and discuss (page 44).

• Introduce and explain Research Project (page 69).

Lesson 3

• Explain Ballads (page 32).

• Introduce the character Robin Hood.

• View a movie version of "Robin Hood" (page 78).

Lesson 4

• Read Chapters 1 and 2 of *Robin Hood of Sherwood Forest*.

• Discuss Characters and Their Characteristics (page 42).

• Compare Robin Hood with other heroes (page 7)

• Continue Research Project.

Lesson 5

• Read Chapter 3.

• Introduce The Art of Butchery (page 47).

• Continue Research Project.

Lesson 6

• Read Chapter 4.

• Draw a map of Sherwood Forest (page 9).

• Work on 1-4 of Questions for Writing and Discussion (page 40).

• Continue Research Project.

Sample Plan *(cont.)*

Lesson 7

• Read Chapters 5 and 6.

• Create a personality portrait of the Sheriff of Nottingham (page 7).

Lesson 8

• Read Chapter 7.

• Do Mathematics in Sherwood Forest (pages 12-13) and Medieval Math (page 46).

• Dramatize parts of the book (page 8).

• Continue Research Project.

Lesson 9

• Read Chapters 8 and 9.

• Do Sequencing and Summary activity (pages 10-11).

• Complete Research Project.

Lesson 10

• Read Chapter 10.

• Share Research Projects.

• Create a new character or adventure (page 8).

• Culminating Activity: Archery Contest and Medieval Festival (pages 64-68).

Overview of Activities

SETTING THE STAGE

1. Preview and choose an appropriate movie for your class to view. Several choices are listed in the bibliography (page 78).

2. Using the recording of the traditional air "Robin Hood and the Stranger" from Joseph Ritsin's *A Collection of Poems, Songs, and Ballads,* 1932, or a theme from a Robin Hood movie, have your students sing together or play the tune on handmade instruments. (Directions for making minstrel's flutes are on page 63.)

3. Share the book *Illuminations* by Jonathan Hunt with the class (bibliography, page 77). This is a very colorful text, made up of intense illustrations. It is an excellent introduction to the vocabulary of the period.

4. Introduce historical characters such as King Henry II, Eleanor of Aquitaine, and their sons, Richard I, Geoffrey, and John I. Refer to bibliography for sources of information about these and other characters.

5. Display a map of England. Locate principal cities and point out places important to the story. Use the map for reference throughout the medieval times unit. Complete the map sizing activity on pages 53-54 with students. Have them graph coordinates to reproduce the map.

6. With a partner, fill in the chart on page 44 comparing life in the Middle Ages to that of the twentieth century. Pose the questions, "In which era would you prefer to live? Why?"

Overview of Activities *(cont.)*

ENJOYING THE BOOK

1. Robin and his men had to hunt and kill their food. Use the butcher's chart on page 47 with students to diagram the parts of a steer and how it would be cut. Research and discuss how meat can be preserved.

2. Make the butcher's chart of the steer (page 48). Have students use the outline of the steer and draw in the parts of meat and where they would be found.

3. Using information from the book, have the students draw a map of Sherwood Forest, illustrating Robin's camp and hiding places (page 9).

4. Introduce your students to the idea of analyzing the characters they are reading about and comparing the characters to themselves. Use the Characters and Their Characteristics activity on page 42 to describe Robin Hood, Will Stutely, and Little John. As an extension, create a personality portrait of the Sheriff of Nottingham and other characters introduced throughout the unit.

Internet Extenders

Medieval History Site Map

http://historymedren.about.com/education/historymedren/library/blsitemap.htm

Summary: Click on graphics to access information about medieval history. These include a map with links to additional information about the medieval times in Europe, Byzantium, Japan, and Russia. Click on the Medieval Life icon (lower left corner) of the map to locate links to A Medieval Christmas and Voices from the Past.

Nottingham, England

http://www.proweb.co.uk/~lordthorpe/nottingham/notts1.htm

Activity Summary: Read the history of Nottingham and then click on the buttons to see the castle, and read about Robin Hood, Will Scarlet, and Little John. Scan down the list of buttons to click on Sherwood Forest. (*Note:* According to the information at this Web site, Robin lived sometime between 1160-1347. The generally accepted dates for his exploits are the period from 1260-1280. Since Richard the Lionhearted was King of England from 1189-1199, this would mean Robin Hood did not live during his reign.)

Robin Hood

http://www.robinhood.ltd.uk/robinhood/index.html

Activity Summary: This Web site is devoted to the legends of Robin Hood. Divide the students into groups and have them visit the Fact or Fiction section. Have each group read a different topic in this section and then present their information, to the class in the order listed. Have them create pictures to enhance their presentation.

Overview of Activities *(cont.)*

ENJOYING THE BOOK *(cont.)*

7. Complete Mathematics in Sherwood Forest (pages 12-13) and Medieval Math (page 46). Assign these as group activities or independent practice. Students can also create their own problems, exchange, and solve.

8. Story comprehension and summary writing are reinforced by student skills in sequencing and summarizing. As an introduction, place the main ideas or events of recently read or more universally known stories on cards and scramble them. Unscramble with students and model summary writing using sequenced main idea cards. Review the meaning and purpose of sequencing and the methods of summarization. Work with students on Sequencing and Summary activity (pages 10-11). Reference to this activity is also made in the *Adam of the Road* section of this thematic unit.

EXTENDING THE BOOK

1. Dramatize parts of *Robin Hood of Sherwood Forest*. The short chapters are ideal for short individual plays. Assign each chapter to a group of 3 to 5 students. The dramatizations can be pantomimed with one student reading a portion of the story.

2. Have students write an additional chapter to the adventures of Robin Hood and/or create a new character to join Robin's band.

3. The research project presented in this unit (page 69) can by introduced at any point. If you have decided to assign the biographical research project in this section of the unit, students could share the reports with the class at this time. Encourage them to use visual aids and other resources they may have prepared when presenting reports.

4. As a culminating activity, hold an archery contest and a medieval festival. Conduct the archery contest (pages 64-65) using children's rubber tipped arrows. Archery and safety rules are provided on these pages. If archery is a physical education activity in your school, see if a P.E. teacher will coordinate activities with your unit. Use *A Medieval Feast* by Aliki (bibliography, page 77) and pages 66-68 to help plan the feast. These activities can be used after reading *Robin Hood of Sherwood Forest,* or at the end of the entire unit.

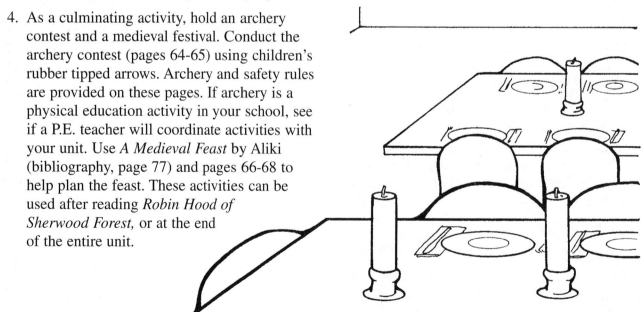

8

Robin Hood's Hideout

The town of Nottingham is located in the center of England, about 125 miles northeast of London. North of Nottingham is Sherwood Forest. It is bordered by the Dove River on the west and the Trent River on the east. The town of Sheffield is to the northeast of Sherwood Forest. The forest is approximately 35 miles wide and 40 miles long.

Use these facts and information from the story to create a map of Sherwood Forest, detailing Robin's hideout and special meeting places.

Sequencing and Summary

The ability to identify important events in daily reading assignments is an essential skill for students. They should be able to place these events in the order in which they occur.

Assignment:

1. Divide the reading of the text into sections that are appropriate for the reading level and attention span of your students.

2. After reading, ask the class to list the most important events of the section read. Narrow the answers down to the five most important events.

3. List them in order.

4. With the class, use the words first, second, third, fourth, and fifth to write the events in order. Have students develop a paragraph from these events, using the following as a model:

   First, Robin got up in the early morning and dressed. Second, he prepared breakfast for his friends. Third, he took his bow and went hunting. Fourth, he shot a deer and carried it to camp. Fifth, he held up a rich noble and returned to camp.

5. Brainstorm alternative words such as *then, after, next,* and *finally,* to introduce the series of events.

6. Rewrite the paragraph using the new words. Discuss how the paragraph sounds. Point out that they have just summarized the main events of the daily reading assignment. Each reading section can be summarized in this way. Summaries may be written by the class as a whole, in small cooperative groups, or individually.

7. Ask the class to suggest other combinations of words which could be used to make a summary concise, easy, and interesting to read. Some suggested words are:

   - First, then, also, next, finally
   - First, next, after, later, last
   - Starting, later, then, also, concluding with
   - At the start, second, next, then, finally

Sequencing Chart

What Happened				
1. **First**	2. **Next**	3. **After that**	4. **Then**	5. **Finally**

10

Sequencing and Summary *(cont.)*

Locating the key events in a story is an important skill. Are you able to retell the events in the order in which they occurred? Can you use sequencing word patterns to make a summary interesting and easy to read?

Unscramble the following paragraph.

Robin Hood of Sherwood Forest—Chapter 1

Match the beginning word with the proper sequence of events.

First	Robin is charged with the crime of killing a king's deer.
Later	He swears to fight unjust laws.
Then	Robin competes with a forester in an archery contest.
Next	Robin escapes into the forest.
Finally	He forms a band of outlaws.

Fill in the blanks in the paragraph with sequencing words to make the events interesting and easy to read.

Robin Hood of Sherwood Forest—Chapter 2

_____ Robin went walking in the woods seeking adventure. _____ Robin

tried to cross a log bridge and met a stranger coming from the opposite direction. _____

Robin and the stranger had words and began to fight with staffs. Robin was knocked off the log.

_____ he was introduced to Little John and they became fast friends.

Reread the order in which things were done. Is it simple and clear? If not, change it. Write a topic sentence for your paragraph to introduce what you've just explained. Combine all into a clearly organized paragraph.

Mathematics in Sherwood Forest

Adventure literature is the perfect vehicle to capture the attention of students and introduce the idea of math as a daily living skill and necessity.

Students can create their own word problems and mathematical calculations to assist Robin Hood in his escapes and adventures.

Using quotes from the text *Robin Hood of Sherwood Forest* (page numbers from the novel are found in parentheses), students can use math to determine depth, length, height, distance, area, and quantity.

1. "After a while, finding no adventure on the road, Robin directed his steps toward a by-path. It led across a brook spanned by a bridge that was no more than a log."
   "No sooner had he started across than he spied a tall stranger coming from the other side. Thinking to cross first, since the log was only wide enough for one and not the other, Robin quickened his steps." (page 13)

   a. Robin had walked 12 feet along the log bridge, and the stranger had walked 12 feet. If Robin and the stranger were facing each other and were exactly 21 feet apart, how long was the bridge?

   b. If the log that the bridge was made of was exactly one-fifth as wide as it was long, how wide was it?

2. " 'Go back, ye giant fellow,' Robin called cheerfully, 'or I'll dampen thy great body in this stream.' The tall stranger took not a backward nor a forward step, but said, 'Nay. Only to a better man than myself will I give way.'
   'Then give way, I say,' said Robin, drawing an arrow from his quiver, 'for I will soon show thee the better man. I have only to bend my bow, and this arrow will hit its mark at thy heart.' " (page 13–14)

   a. Robin's bow was a full 54 inches in height. If the bow, with one point resting on the ground, reached Robin's chest and if from Robin's chest to the crown of his head measured 18 inches long, how tall was he?

3. " 'The goose will soon be browning on the fire,' said Midge, 'and as everyone knows, a fine goose dinner is worth much—ten gold pieces, I'd say.' " (page 79)

   a. If a gold piece is worth $5.00, how much does a goose dinner cost?

   b. It takes 6 goose dinners to feed all of the merry men. How many gold pieces must Midge find in order to feed them?

Mathematics in Sherwood Forest *(cont.)*

4. "Allan looked at the five score of brawny men about him." (page 83)

   a. A score is a set of 20. How many men are there in five score?

   b. London Bridge was built between 1176 and 1209. How many score is this? (Round off to the nearest score.)

5. "Robin took a step back in surprise, for the stranger was at least seven feet tall - a good foot taller than Robin Hood - and his leg was in truth as thick as Robin's waist." (page 14)

   How tall is Robin Hood?

6. "For forty days, Robin Hood and his men were free to roam the length and breadth of England as King Henry had promised. Then came the forty-first day and the forty-second, and in all the days that followed they were free." (page 113)

   a. How many weeks are there in 42 days?

   b. If 1/7 of the way through their wanderings Robin Hood and his men decided to camp on the outskirts of Sherwood forest, on which day would they have camped?

7. "In an instant there came running twoscore bold men, dressed in Lincoln green, their bows drawn tight." (page 118-119)

   a. How many men are in twoscore?

   b. If these men were joined by 3 score and 7 more, how many men came running altogether?

As an extension, ask students to create math problems from their own reading and distribute to classmates to solve.

Adam of the Road
by Elizabeth Jane Gray
Summary

Eleven-year-old Adam Quartermayne leaves the Abbey of St. Alban and sets out on the road of Old England with his father Roger, a famous minstrel, and Nick, his cocker spaniel. Adam and his father head for the faire of St. Giles in Winchester. Nick is stolen. Adam chases the thief and is separated from his father for several more months. Adam's search for Nick and his father introduces the reader to medieval life in England while giving a detailed account of life in 13th century.

This outline is a suggested plan for using the various activities that are presented in this book. You should adapt these ideas to fit your own classroom situation and the ability level of your students.

Sample Plan

Lesson 1

• Discuss the time and setting of the story. Introduce the feudal system (pages 50-52), and the minstrel's life (page 32).

• Read "Adam."

• Start a time line (page 16).

• Begin a daily diary of Adam's adventures (page 16).

Lesson 2

• Read "Nick."

• Do daily diary entry.

• Begin plotting Adam's journey (page 16).

Lesson 3

• Read "Roger." Introduce Cinquains (page 19).

Lesson 4

• Read "The Road."

• Continue diary.

• List characteristics of Adam and Nick. (page 7)

• Answer discussion questions 1-6 (page 22).

Lesson 5

• Read "Going to London."

• Design a story pyramid (page 41).

Lesson 6

• Read "A Blush of Boys."

• Continue diary.

• Discuss comparisons of "London Bridge" (page 38).

Lesson 7

• Read "Jankin" and "Red in the Morning."

• Write a cinquain about a main character (page 17)

Lesson 8

• Read "Night in Westhumble Lane" and "Here, Nick!"

• Create a cinquain about an animal in the story (page 18).

• Update the time line and map of Adam's journey.

• Update your diary entries of Adam's adventures.

Sample Plan

Lesson 9

- Read "Adam Swims the Wey" and "The Ferryman's House."

- Answer questions 7-11 (page 22).

- Construct a model of the streets of London (page 17).

- Continue diary entries.

Lesson 10

- Read "Arrows in the King's Forest" and "Adam to the Rescue." Answer question 12 (page 22).

- Continue construction project.

Lesson 11

- Read "St. Giles Fair" and "The Fall of Adam."

- Answer question 13 (page 22).

- Update your diary, time line, and map.

Lesson 12

- Read "Adam Meets some Minstrels" and "Hue and Cry."

- Make a Medieval Daisy Chain (page 23).

- Update diaries.

Lesson 13

- Read "News of Roger" and "What Have You Done With Him?"

- Construct Minstrel's Flute (page 63).

- Update your diary, time line and map.

- Discuss the Christmas celebration (page 17).

Lesson 14

- Read "Adam's Song" and "Adam Helps a Plowman."

- Do the *Adam of the Road* Crossword (page 21)

- Update diary, time line and map.

Lesson 15

- Read "Loud Sing Cuckoo!" Answer questions 14-17 (page 22).

- Use Sequencing and Summary (page 11) to write a summary of the story.

- Make a banner or mural showing Adam's travels (page 62).

Overview of Activities

SETTING THE STAGE

1. Discuss the purpose and life of the minstrel. Refer to "The Singer of Ballads" on page 32.

2. Review a map of England and its capital city.

3. Explain the feudal system (pages 50-52). Review the definition of each word and the flow chart. Help students make comparisons between present day systems of society and the feudal system.

Overview of Activities *(cont.)*

ENJOYING THE BOOK

1. Students will visualize the journey and relate to Adam more easily by using a map of England and plotting Adam's search for Nick and his father. Add creativity by illustrating important events along the way.

2. Let students keep a daily diary of Adam's travel and adventures. The diary may be written from the point of view of Adam or another character in the story. Multiple copies of the diary worksheet (page 45) can be made into student books in which to log daily entries. Students may wish to make a cover for their diary.

3. After reading "The Road to London," have students read a version of "London Bridge" (page 38). Many of them will remember the childhood song. Discuss it and have students read it chorally.

4. Create a time line showing the journeys and adventures that Adam encountered along the way to Oxford. This can be displayed and used as a reference tool.

Internet Extenders

The Middle Ages

http://www.learner.org/exhibits/middleages/

Activity Summary: This is one of the best Web sites for students on the Middle Ages. The home page has a brief description of the Middle Ages. Students should click on Enter after reading this introduction. This will take them to information on the feudal life and lists of other areas of this Web site to visit that describe religion, homes, clothing, health, arts and entertainment, and town life. With each topic there is a link to more details and sometimes an activity. An example of this is the Art and Entertainment site. Readers can click on Try Your Luck as a Medieval Musician or follow the Story Weaver to see a tapestry of medieval times and write a story about it. There is also a list of stories written by others who looked at the tapestry. Groups of students could be assigned to investigate each topic and then report back what they have learned.

Camelot Village

http://www.camelotintl.com/village/

Activity Summary: Read the brief description of the Middle Ages and then click on The Camelot International Village link to learn more about the people and the society of the Middle Ages. Click on the pictures of the lord, thief, trader, woman, peasant, knight, and entertainer who will describe such things as the feudal system, punishment, and how to live like a lord.

Overview of Activities *(cont.)*

ENJOYING THE BOOK *(cont.)*

5. Introduce the poetic verse of cinquains. Refer to page 19 and use the cinquain format. Have students write about a minstrel or life in the Middle Ages. Let them write a few cinquains as a class and read them chorally.

   As an extension, have students write a cinquain about one of the main characters. Making a character web or using Characters and Their Characteristics (page 42) may provide ideas for cinquains.

6. Discuss the characteristics an individual may possess. Refer to Characters and Their Characteristics (page 42). In small groups ask students to find and list appropriate characteristics for Adam and Nick. Compare and discuss class responses.

7. As a creative writing project, have students add another chapter to the novel. Students may create their own titles or choose from the following: Adam Becomes a Knight, Adam Saves High's Life, Nick Becomes a Hero, Adam Becomes Mayor of London, Escape from the Castle Dungeon.

8. To enhance the story setting, build a cardboard construction of the streets of London as they are described in the story. (For the person who doesn't wish to start from scratch or who needs a model to follow, Usborne Cut-out Models Make This Model Village is a kit for constructing a medieval village.)

9. Have the students visit the Web sites about castles (page 58) and the Crusades (page 59).

Internet Extender

Christmas Feast in the Middle Ages

http://www.byu.edu/ipt/projects/middleages/LifeTimes/Christmas.html

Summary: Adam spent a lonely Christmas at the deLisle's home. Visit this Web site to see how the celebration of Christmas was observed in the Middle Ages and how it evolved.

Overview of Activities *(cont.)*

EXTENDING THE BOOK

1. In medieval times the daisy was used as part of a head decoration. Have students make daisy chains, following the directions on page 23.

2. As the minstrels moved about singing songs of love and tales of the knights, they often accompanied themselves on instruments like the lute, harp or violin. Students will enjoy making the minstrel's flute on page 63. When completed, they can learn a few simple songs on their flutes and provide entertainment for the class or during the festival.

3. The story pyramid is a helpful technique in character, story, setting, and plot development. Use the story pyramid on page 41 with the class. Then have students work in groups or pairs to design a story pyramid for *Adam of the Road*.

4. For vocabulary and content review, have students complete the *Adam of the Road* crossword (page 21).

5. Help students identify and sequence important events by following the same procedure as in Robin Hood activity (Sequencing and Summary, page 11). Students can use these to develop a summary of the book.

6. The author features animals throughout the book. Have students write cinquains about one of the animals in the story and illustrate them. Prepare a bulletin board on which to display animal cinquains. For a review of cinquains refer to page 19.

7. In *Adam of the Road*, Adam is very attached to his dog Nick. When Nick is stolen, Adam has many adventures while trying to recover his beloved pet. Take a survey in your class. Find out who has a dog. Ask if any students would go through what Nick did to get his pet back.

Talk about the history of dogs. Dogs belong to the family of animals known as Canidae. The history of this family can be traced back about forty million years. The earliest ancestor of our trusted friend and pet was called Miacis (my-ay-sis) and looked more like a weasel than a dog. From this ancient animal came the dog and its modern day "cousins," the wolf, jackal, fox, raccoon, and bear. Throughout history dogs have been a part of people's lives. Balto was an Eskimo dog who, in 1925, led a dog team 650 miles to deliver diphtheria serum. Barry was a St. Bernard who rescued 40 people who were lost in Switzerland in the 1800s.

Ask students to find out more about dogs and share the information with the class. Some areas for investigation include dog care, grooming, exercise, and medical attention.

18

Cinquains

A cinquain is a special type of poem consisting of five lines. Two kinds of cinquains, the word cinquain and the formal cinquain, are shown on this page.

After reading the poems, write two word cinquains and two formal cinquains about the Middle Ages. From the four cinquains you have written, choose your favorite and share it with your classmates by reading it or publishing it in a school newsletter.

Word cinquain pattern

Line 1- one word which states the subject

Line 2 - two words which describe the subject

Line 3 - three words which express action

Line 4 - a four word phrase which expresses a feeling

Line 5 - one word which is a synonym for the subject in line 1

Examples of word cinquains:

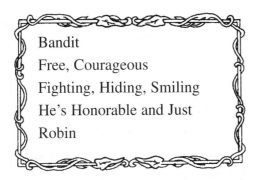

Bandit
Free, Courageous
Fighting, Hiding, Smiling
He's Honorable and Just
Robin

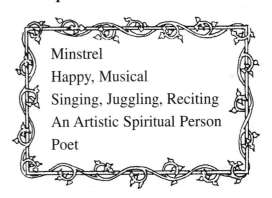

Minstrel
Happy, Musical
Singing, Juggling, Reciting
An Artistic Spiritual Person
Poet

Formal cinquain pattern

Line 1—two syllables

Line 2—four syllables

Line 3—six syllables

Line 4—eight syllables

Line 5—wo syllables

An example of a formal cinquain:

Minstrel

Wandering man

Creative, happy, free

Lonely, single, homeless, alone

Roaming

Adam of the Road

Missing Animal Report

After searching unsuccessfully for his stolen dog Nick, Adam realizes he needs help in tracking him down. Adam has come to you for assistance.

Use the information from _Adam of the Road_ to fill in the missing animal report that will help Adam locate his lost pet.

Missing Animal Report

Animal's name_____

Owner _____

Physical description of the animal

_____

_____

_____

Personality description of the animal

_____

_____

_____

Picture of Missing Animal

Describe where you last saw the animal

_____

_____

List those who know the animal

_____   _____

_____   _____

_____   _____

Animal prints (paws, tracks, etc.)

Report Filed by: _____   Date: _____

Directions: Use the clues below to fill in the puzzle. Those with asterisks (*) are related to *Adam of the Road.*

Across

1. City of famous college*
4. Jellies and_____
7. _____of the Road*
8. Ruler of the manor*
9. Preposition
10. Adam's best friend*
11. Post script: Abbreviation
12. Upon
14. Subject Adam studied*
15. Opposite of out
16. Opposite of from
17. Opposite of off
18. Feline
20. Masculine pronoun
21. Roger's occupation*
23. A type of material
24. Either _____
25. Opposite of under
26. To talk with music
29. Produced by a hen
30. Past tense of eat
31. Portions*
34. A score minus nine*
36. _____ Humbug!
38. _____, myself, and I.
39. Roger's horse*

Down

1. Single
2. Place where Adam hid*
3. _____ Ellen took care of Nick for Adam*
4. _____ steals Adam's dog*
5. I'm = I _____
6. Present tense of sat
9. One more
10. Writing instrument
11. Cooking utensil
13. Christmas
14. The first place Adam visits*
15. It is = _____
19. Insects
21. Combine
22. Adam's father*
23. What you walk with
27. One who is greedy is self___
28. Light fog*
31. Male child
32. Where Adam received his education*
33. Used to cross a river*
35. Doctors who care for pets
37. Musical instrument*
38. The month Adam's story begins*

Discussion Questions for *Adam of the Road*

Use these questions to spark discussions, create interest in the book, and as writing starters.

1. When and where does the story begin?

2. What has been Adam's dream since Easter?

3. What did minstrels do? What instrument did Adam play?

4. Who were Adam's two closest companions?

5. When Sir Edmund approached the abbey, Adam began to do tricks. What tricks did he do? What tricks do children do today?

6. The next morning Adam turned cartwheels for joy. Why? Why was he also sad?

7. What was the road to London like? What do you think the roads are like today?

8. What section in the story tells you about plumbing in the 13th century? Describe it.

9. What is the quintain? What was tilting? What was the practice for? What other sports did Adam and the other boys do? What sports do you enjoy?

10. Through gambling, Roger lost Bayard to Jankin. What concerns did Adam have for Bayard? Do people mistreat animals today? What organizations prevent cruelty to animals?

11. Describe the streets of London, then and now.

12. As the story goes on, Adam becomes lost and joins a merchant's group. What happens to the group in the King's Forest? How did Adam help catch the robbers?

13. What happens to Adam while he is watching a miracle play? Why is it called a miracle play?

14. Adam found Nick and his old school friend Perkin on Perkin's family farm. Adam helped with the farm so that Perkin could go to school. What does this show about Adam's character?

15. Was Adam polite when the miller gave him bagpipes? Why?

16. Do you think Adam remained a minstrel the rest of his life? Why?

17. What qualities did Adam have that might make him a good knight if he had the chance?

22

Medieval Daisy Chains

In the Middle Ages people decorated their heads with flowers and leaves. This is fun to do with daisies when they are in bloom in the spring or early summer, but any flower with a long stem will do. The daisy is a wild flower, and can frequently be seen growing along the sides of country roads.

Materials:

scissors

freshly picked daisies with long stems, or silk flowers

butter knife

paper clips or thin pieces of wire

wire cutters (for silk flowers)

Directions (for live flowers):

1. Cut daisies, leaving a stem that is about 6" (15 cm) long.

2. Cut a small slit through all the stems starting about 1" (2 cm) from the bottom. Cut up toward the flower to make sure you do not cut all the way through the bottom of the stem.

3. Pass the stem of one daisy through the slit of another. Pull the second stem all the way through the first. This must be done carefully so the stems are not broken or torn.

4. Take a third daisy and pass it through the slit of the second daisy.

5. Continue until you have a chain of daisies.

6. When the chain is as long as you want, attach the last stem to the stem of the first daisy with a small paper clip or piece of wire.

   (If fresh flowers are not readily available, silk flowers may be substituted. However the stems will need to be tied together with small twists of thin wire.)

The Door in the Wall
by Marguerite de Angeli
Summary

Robin is a knight's son. During the time of the Black Plague in London, Robin falls ill and loses the use of his legs. His father is fighting at the king's side in the Scottish wars; his mother is in the queen's service. Robin must now serve as a page at Lindsay Castle as the first step toward knighthood. He is taken to a monastery by Brother Luke who teaches him to use his head and hands wisely. Robin finally reaches Lindsay Castle, where his courage and resourcefulness win the king's recognition. The family is reunited on Christmas Day.

This outline is a suggested plan for using the various activities that are presented in this book. You should adapt these ideas to fit your own classroom situation and the ability level of your students.

Sample Plan

Lesson 1

• Discuss the 14th century and the Bubonic Plague (page 25).

• Begin reading *The Door in the Wall*, pages 7–18.

• Create a Coat of Arms for Robin's family (page 27).

Lesson 2

• Read pages 18–31.

• Review Character and Their Characteristics (page 42).

• Design soft plaster carvings (page 29).

Lesson 3

• Read pages 32–41.

• Do Comparison Chart of medieval times and today (page 44).

• Answer discussion questions 1–3 (page 31).

• Complete the soft plaster carvings.

Lesson 4

• Read pages 42–52.

• Begin writing plays.

• Compare meals then and now (page 25),

• Design a medieval town and castle (page 58),

Lesson 5

• Read pages 53–61.

• Conduct a chess and checker tournament (page 25).

• Continue writing of plays.

• Answer discussion questions 4–11 (page 31).

• Write letters from Robin (page 26).

Lesson 6

• Read pages 62–85.

• Share decorative letter samples (page 73).

• Make Very Berry Ink (page 49).

Sample Plan

Lesson 7

• Read pages 86–103.

• Play Blindman's Bluff (page 25).

• Design shop signs or banners (page 26).

Lesson 8

• Read pages 104–121.

• Complete discussion questions 12–13 (page 31).

• Perform plays.

Overview of Activities

SETTING THE STAGE

1. *The Door in the Wall* takes place during a time when the Bubonic Plague, also called the Black Death, destroyed about one-fourth of Europe's population. The disease, usually transmitted by fleas from infected rats, caused black spots to appear under the skin. The lymph glands, or *buboes* (from which the term bubonic was derived), became swollen. Other symptoms such as fever, chills, and headache accompanied the sudden attack of this disease. Discuss why the disease spread as it did. Compare modern medicine to that in the Middle Ages.

2. Read aloud *A Medieval Feast* by Aliki.

3. Display a wall map of Great Britain. Have students locate London, England and Scotland. Discuss the war with Scotland and other places mentioned in the book. Have students locate these places on individual copies of the map.

ENJOYING THE BOOK

1. Compare the meals eaten at the castle with what the peasants ate. Compare both to what you eat. Make a chart of similarities and differences. If students are familiar with food groups, evaluate the quality of each type of diet.

2. Create a coat of arms for Robin's family. Design one for your family. The activity on page 28 will assist students in developing unique designs.

3. Hoodman's Blind and Blindman's Bluff had their origins in the Middle Ages. Play Blindman's Bluff. Choose one player to be "it." Blindfold and spin "it" around. While blindfolded, let "it" try to tag another player who then becomes "it."

4. Conduct a round robin chess and/or checker tournament in your classroom. You could involve the entire grade level and make this an ongoing activity.

5. Make a chart comparing life in medieval times with life today. The following problems can be included: removing stains; getting rid of insects; telling time; having teeth fixed; getting news; producing farm tools; receiving medical care; getting an education; entertainment; printing books; making clothes; making shoes; heating a home; preparing food.

Overview of Activities *(cont.)*

ENJOYING THE BOOK *(cont.)*

6. Design a shop sign or banner that doesn't use words or letters. (Guilds had banners with emblems showing tools of the trade.) Most people could not read or write, so signs had to deliver a message without using words. Some suggested signs are *Barber Shop, Shoemaker, Pharmacy, Baker, Blacksmith,* and *Carpenter.*

7. Similarities and differences in ourselves and people of long ago enhance our understanding of the past. Compare a monk's life with your own. Make a time chart of each.

8. Distribute decorative letters (page 73). Have students practice making the letters by giving them free-flowing ink pens to practice printing. Have them design a page as the monks did. (*Illuminations* provides excellent examples.)

9. Before reading Robin's letter to his parents, have students pretend they are Robin and write the letter. Students can share their letters in small groups and then compare them to the letter Robin writes.

10. In the story, John and Alan are sometimes referred to as John-go-in-the-Wynd and Alan-at-Gate. Have students interpret how John and Alan got these names. List characters from other common stories and give them special names as well. This can be done collectively, in small groups, or individually.

11. Develop class definitions for characters and characteristics, using the activity on page 42. Make a list of characteristics to describe Robin, Brother Luke, and John and display in a chart for comparison and/or future reference.

12. Robin learns to carve while he is recuperating. The activity on page 29 gives students the opportunity to experience the art of carving. Display finished carvings.

Internet Extenders

Black Death

http://www.discovery.com/stories/history/blackdeath/blackdeath.html

Activity Summary: In the 14th century a plague spread across Asia, Europe, and Great Britain with such virulence that the course of human history changed forever. Leave the present day and travel back 600 years to witness this crucial moment when many believed the end of the world had come. Click on the rat to begin your journey. Click on the map to read about the stories from various cities to which the plague spread. Click Transcript to read personal accounts.

The Black Death

http://history.idbsu.edu/westciv/plague/

Summary: This online textbook describes details of the plague, including quotes from people of the time and the information of the physical effects of the disease. (Note: Teachers should check this Web site to determine if it is appropriate for their students.)

Coat of Arms

In the Middle Ages, knights and royalty displayed symbols on the shields they carried in battle and displayed around the castle. Banners, shields, and crests revealed the characteristics of the person or family.

- Shields may be divided into halves, quarters, or thirds. The divisions do not need to be exact but should be balanced.

- Marks of cadency (the descent of a younger branch from the mainline of a family) were used to distinguish the sons of a particular family.

Oldest—file or label	**Fourth**—martlet	**Seventh**—rose
Second—crescent	**Fifth**—annulet	**Eighth**—cross moline
Third—the mullet	**Sixth**—fleur-de-lis	**Ninth**—octofoil

- Lions were a favorite symbol of the English. They were shown in four positions.
  Rampant: lion standing on hind feet ready to climb.
  Couchant: lion lying down with head raised.
  Passant: lion walking with distant forepaw raised.
  Statant: lion standing on four legs.

- Other symbols that you may want to use include the following:
  Crescent: victory over adversity; always shown with horns pointed upward.
  Eagle: strength of mind; shown with wings spread.
  Falcon: bravery; shown looking to the right of the shield.
  Griffin: valor and vigilance; half-eagle, half-lion mythological beast.
  Hand: generosity—open hand; strength—closed hand.
  Leopard: wisdom and agility; sometimes shown walking toward the right, but usually only shown as a full face.
  Stag: purity and strength of spirit; usually shown with one foot up.
  Pheon: speed and directness; head of an arrow.
  Sun: splendor and royalty; usually shows a face of the sun.
  Heart: loyalty and love; sometimes shown pierced by an arrow.
  Tower: strength and protection; symbol of defense.

My Coat of Arms

Use the shield below to create your own coat of arms. Divide your shield into sections. Use the symbols on page 27 or make up your own to show what's special about you.

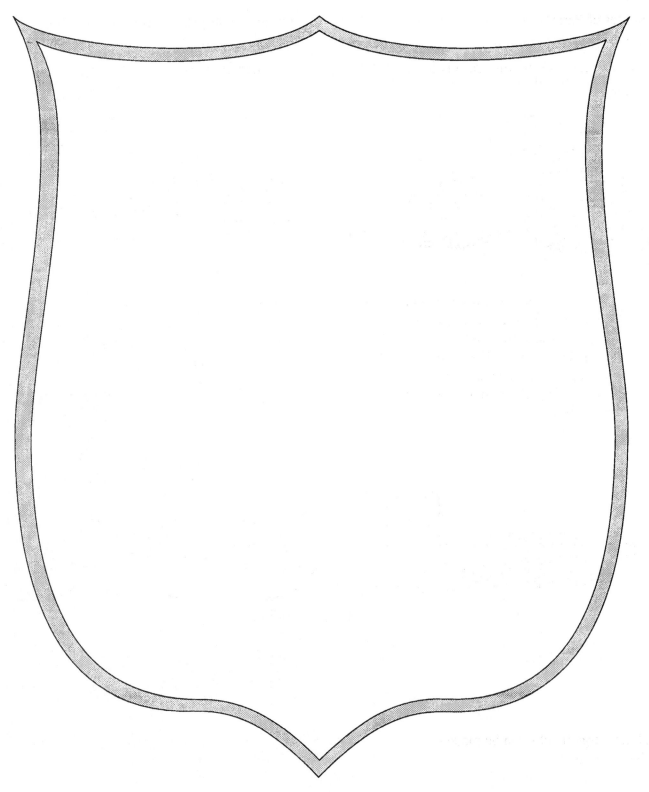

Plaster Block Carvings

This activity enables students to experience the art of carving. In *The Door in the Wall*, Robin learns to carve as a means of earning his way and as a therapy while he is recuperating.

Materials:

plaster of Paris

milk cartons or shoe boxes

kitchen tools or sculpture chisels or metal files

water

vegetable oil or petroleum jelly

container for mixture

salt, coffee grounds, vermiculite (optional)

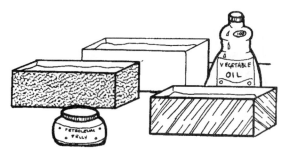

1. Mix plaster of Paris, following package directions. A little salt added to the plaster mix will speed the thickening. Coffee grounds or vermiculite added to the plaster mix makes an interesting easy-to-carve texture. Experimenting with different quantities of each added to the plaster mix will make a great science experiment.

2. Coat the milk cartons with petroleum jelly or vegetable oil to prevent plaster from sticking to the mold. Pour mixed plaster of Paris into milk cartons or shoe boxes, depending on how big a carving block you want. It is best to rinse the plastic bowls and buckets immediately. Plaster will clog the sink drains. Dump it outside and dilute it with lots of water.

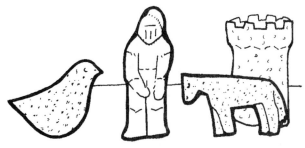

3. When plaster is set, and no longer warm, tear off the box.

4. You can carve the block with kitchen tools or sculpture chisels. A plaster block dipped in water is easier to carve. Do not dip it too often or for too long.

Note: Large blocks can be made to build up a form then filed and sanded to create a larger structure like a castle.

Word Shield Word Hunt

Locate the words listed below on the word shield. They may be listed vertically, horizontally, or diagonally.

The Door in the Wall	Westminster	Mother	Lunch
London	Fog	Sheepskin	Jenny
Marguerite de Angeli	Sir	Luke	Millicent
Patience	Horse	Robin	Jousting
Crutch	Mist	Friar	Urchin
Devotion	Dame	Scottish wars	Ten
Knight	Parchment	Armor	Whittle
Windhole	Fishmonger	Castle	D'Ath
Robbers	Cat	Bells	

```
A M O T H E R D E V O T I O N S C
M H A W E S T M I N S T E R B H A
A T H H B O Y O P S H E E O P E T
R D W I N D H O L E O F R B A E E
G P A T I E N C A K R R T B D P P
U A R T O R F O G N S I S E A S A
E T M L U K E R U I E A G R D K T
R A R E N S I R E G S R T S E I E
I T B U D C D V E H A N T D F N N
T H E D O O R I N T H E W A L L C
E G L I J T H O T N E R A M O O E
D H L D A T H O B E L N E E P N M
E R S Y N I T N F I N G B K N D I
A T U W N S K L M O N P E Y S O L
N R O N I H D O W L U R C H I N L
G S M M E W A L E L O R T H I N I
E D T O M A P L C R U T C H E J C
L A B C R R T J O U S T I N G E E
I F I R S S E P A T I E N C E N N
E D C B A F I S H M O N G E R N T
P A R C H M E N T C L U N C H Y Z
```

30

Discussion Questions for
The Door in the Wall

1. Feudalism was a special social system. How was it different from our way of living?

2. Compare the life of a serf with the life of a tenant farmer.

3. Compare our personal rights with those of feudal peasants, knights, and kings.

4. What was it like to live in a castle?

5. What were the guilds? Who belonged to them? Why were they started?

6. What were some advantages to belonging to a guild?

7. How are modern-day labor unions similar to medieval guilds? How are they different?

8. What were some of the services and benefits that monasteries provided for the people? Who provides these services today?

9. Compare your meals with those eaten in the castles. What did the peasants eat?

10. What was a medieval town like? What were the streets like?

11. What were some of the dangers travelers faced when they went from town to town or from castle to castle?

12. Describe the steps that a boy went through to become a knight. Compare the life of a page with the life of a serf's son.

13. Outline the typical day in a monk's life. Compare it to your daily schedule.

The Singers of Ballads

The troubadours or minstrels were the first ones in Western Europe who really thought of love the way we do now, as a one-to-one relationship. They were originally the nobility of Provence and then spread to other parts of France and Europe in the twelfth century. In Germany they were known as the Minnesingers or singers of love. They were the poets of their age. In the Middle Ages the only form of marriage sanctioned by the church was that which was arranged by the family and society. The minstrel's idea of a real one-to-one love was a very dangerous one.

Minstrels sometimes traveled and gave shows to people in the villages. Some entertained at castles, while others belonged to the houses of kings and nobles. Minstrels sang the same ballads and folk tales over and over again, helping to preserve them. With the invention of the printing press in the 1400s, minstrels lost their popularity.

Ballads

A ballad is a song that tells a story in rhyming verse. Most ballads have four-line stanzas of short phrases and an ABAB rhyme scheme. Here is an example from the story *Adam of the Road.*

The highway is the minstrel's home.	A
He's working when he's playing.	B
He's never lost if far he roam.	A
He wanders when he's staying.	B

Because ballads were sung over and over again by different minstrels, they often changed in the telling. They also told and preserved history. The art form of the ballad has survived and is still used to tell stories in song and verse.

The four volumes of Bertrand H. Bronson's *Traditional Tunes of the Child Ballads* (Princeton Univ. Press, 1962) are a good source for standard ballads.

Internet Extender

Medieval Music

http://www.s-hamilton.k12.ia.us/antiqua/instrumt.html

Activity Summary: Have students visit this Web site to learn about 32 different medieval and Renaissance musical instruments. Let them choose several to click on to see pictures and a description of the instruments. Some, such as the dulcimer and bladder pipe, produce sounds as well when you click on the picture of the instrument.

Activities for Using Ballads

Use these activities with your class to teach about ballads.

1. Introduce ballads to the class. Share the information about minstrels and ballads on page 32. Point out that Roger in *Adam of the Road* was a minstrel.

2. If possible obtain recordings of folk songs and play them for the class. Some that would be suitable include "John Henry," "Henry Martin," "Mary Hamilton," and "Barbara Allen" (*Joan Baez Ballad Book,* Vanguard, 1972).

3. Before introducing "Lord Randal" review the following vocabulary from the poem: greenwood—forest; fain—gladly; eels—fish with a snake like body; "Gat your leaving"—got the leftover food; kye—cow. Let students find examples of other words whose meaning can easily be determined by the context such as mak—make or gat—got.

4. Read "Lord Randal" with the class. One effective way to do this is to have one student read the lines of the mother and another read the lines of Lord Randal. Before any student reads out loud, give them time to practice, since the words may be unfamiliar to them.

5. After reading "Lord Randal" ask if students can think of a folk song about a mother having a conversation with her son about a girl. Tell them that one such song is "Billy Boy" (*Tom Glazer's Treasury of Songs for Children,* bibliography, page 77). This song first appeared in the late 1700s in England and Scotland, and is related to "Lord Randal." Sing "Billy Boy." Talk about the similarities between the two.

6. Use comprehension questions on page 36 to spark discussion about "Lord Randal." It is often helpful to have students write answers to those questions that you wish to discuss before you talk about them.

7. Let the students hear a recording of "Barbara Allen." A version sung by Joan Baez is available on "Joan Baez, Vol. 2" (Vanguard, 1987). Then read the version found on page 35 to the class. Ask them what the following words mean: rase—raised; nigh—near, within sight of; dinna—don't; healths—toasts for good fortune; adieu—goodbye, farewell; oter—over; knellin'—to ring in a slow way; shun—keep away from. After reviewing the definitions, have them write sentences using the words from "Barbara Allen."

8. Make sure students are comfortable with the vocabulary of the ballad. Do a choral reading of it.

9. Assign students to answer the comprehension questions for "Barbara Allen" individually. Use the answers as a group discussion.

10. After reading both "Lord Randal" and " Barbara Allen," do the comparison on page 37. Students may work in small groups to write a related scene for a contemporary dramatic television show.

11. Many students remember singing nursery rhymes as young children. Choose a few and review them with your class. Then introduce the nursery rhyme "London Bridge." Explain that London Bridge was originally built from 1176 to 1200 and was used during the Middle Ages to get to London. (See page 38.) The poem is a narrative ballad and has undergone current changes with the move of the original London Bridge to Lake Havasu, Arizona.

12. Students can create their own ballads by writing stories in verse and sharing them with classmates. Use the activity on page 39 to help them with this.

"Lord Randal"

"O where ha you been, Lord Randal, my son?
And where ha you been, my handsome young man?"
"I ha veen at the greenwood; mother, mak my bed soon,
For I'm wearied wi hunting, and fain wad lie down."
"An wha met ye there, Lord Randal, my son?
An wha met you there, my handsome young man?"
"O I met wi my true-love; mother, mak my bed soon,
For I'm wearied wi huntin, and fain wad lie down."
"And what did she give you, Lord Randal, my son?
And what did she give you, my handsome young man?"
"Eels fried in a pan; mother, mak my bed soon,
For I'm wearied wi hunting, and fain wad lie down."
"And wha gat your leavins, Lord Randal, my son?
And wha gat your leavins, my handsome young man?"
"My hawks and my hounds; mother, mak my bed soon,
For I'm wearied wi hunting, and fain wad lie down."
"And what becam of them, Lord Randal, my son?
And what becam of them, my handsome young man?"
"They scretched their legs out an died; mother, mak my bed soon,
For I'm wearied wi huntin, and fain wad lie down."
"O I fear you are poisoned, Lord Randal, my son!
I fear you are poisoned, my handsome young man!"
"O yes, I am poisoned; mother, mak my bed soon,
For I'm sick at the heart, and I fain wad lie down."
"What d'ye leave to your mother, Lord Randal, my son?
What d'ye leave to your mother, my handsome young man?"
"Four and twenty milk kye; mother, mak my bed soon,
For I'm sick at the heart, and I fain wad lie down."
"What'd ye leave to your sister, Lord Randal, my son?
What d'ye leave to your sister, my handsome young man?"
"My gold and my silver; mother, mak my bed soon,
For I'm sick at the heart, and I fain wad lie down."
"What d'ye leave to your brother, Lord Randal, my son?
What d'ye leave to your brother, my handsome young man?"
"My houses and my lands; mother, mak my bed soon,
For I'm sick at the heart, and I fain wad lie down. "
"What d'ye leave to your true-love, Lord Randal, my son?
What d'ye leave to your true-love, my handsome young man?"
"I leave her poison and fire; mother, make my bed soon,
For I'm sick at the heart, and I fain wad lie down."

—Anonymous

"Barbara Allen"

In scarlet town, where I was born, There was a fair maid dwellin', Made every youth cry Well-a-way! Her name was Barbara Allen.

All in the merry month of May When green buds they were swellin', Young Jemmy Grove on his death-bed lay, For love of Barbara Allen.

He sent his man in to her then, To the town where she was dwellin', "O haste and come to my master dear, If your name be Barbara Allen."

So slowly, slowly rase she up, And slowly she came nigh him, And when she drew the curtain by "Young man, I think you're dyin."

"O it's I'm sick and very very sick, And it's all for Barbara Allen." "O the better for me ye'se never be, Tho' your heart's blood were a-spillin!"

"O dinna ye mind young man," says she, "When the red wine ye were fillin, That ye made the healths go round and round, And slighted Barbara Allen?"

He turn'd his face unto the wall, And death was with him dealin': "Adieu, adieu, my dear friends all And be kind to Barbara Allen!"

As she was walking oter the fields, She heard the dead-bell knellin'; And every jow the dead-bell gave Cried "Woe to Barbara Allen."

"O mother, mother, make my bed, O make it soft and narrow: My love had died for me today, I'll die for him tomorrow.

"Farewell," she said, " ye maidens all, And shun the fault I fell in: Henceforth take warning by the fall Of cruel Barbara Allen."

—Anonymous

Comprehension Questions

To help students better understand "Lord Randal" and "Barbara Allen," have them answer these questions. They may work in small groups or individually.

"Lord Randal"

1. There are two characters or speakers in this poem. Who are they?

2. What makes us think that one of the speakers is Randal's mother?

3. What has happened to start the conversation that is taking place?

4. What are some things that you can tell about Lord Randal?

5. What can you tell about Randal's mother?

6. When does his mother know that Randal has been poisoned?

7. What is Lord Randal doing in the last four stanzas?

8. Who is thought to have poisoned Lord Randal?

9. Where had he met his true love?

10. What did Randal leave his true-love in his will?

11. How do you think his mother felt about his bequest to his true love? Give reasons or examples to back up your opinion.

12. What do you think Randal wants to do most of all? Give reasons for your opinion.

As a challenge have students find and compare some of the many versions of "Lord Randal."

"Barbara Allen"

1. Who are the characters in the story?

2. At what time of year does the story take place?

3. Who is the "master" referred to in stanza three?

4. What is "his man" and what has he been sent to do?

5. How would you describe the character of Barbara Allen?

6. How would you summarize the story up to the fourth stanza?

7. In the sixth stanza, why does Barbara Allen speak to the dying man this way? What does she mean by her speech? What is her attitude like?

8. What happens in the seventh stanza?

9. Jemmy says, "Be kind to Barbara Allen!" Why?

10. What happens to Barbara Allen on her way home?

11. What is the fault that Barbara Allen speaks of having fallen into?

12. Predict what will happen the next day.

"Barbara Allen" and "Lord Randal" Comparison

1. First, take a look at the layout of the two ballads.
   a. What do they have in common?
   b. What is different?

2. Look at the characters in the story.
   a. What do they have in common?
   b. What makes them different?

3. Describe the characters Barbara Allen and Lord Randal.

4. What subject is discussed in both ballads?

5. Think of the situations that occurred with Barbara Allen and Lord Randal. Decide whether you would have done the same thing as he/she did and tell us what you might have done.

6. Would you characterize the main character as good or bad? Give reasons.

7. How do these ballads relate to contemporary life?

8. How are each of these ballads like a soap opera on television?

9. As a small group, work together to write a scene from a contemporary dramatic show using one of the ballads as the basis for your script.

10. You are to interview Lord Randal or Barbara Allen for a newspaper or interview show. What questions would you ask each of them?

11. Have another classmate play the role of Barbara Allen or Lord Randal and conduct the interview. Then write a news article. Be sure to cover the who, what, when, where, why, and how in your interview and article.

"London Bridge"

Mother Goose rhymes have been repeated, elaborated, created and changed to fit the times by children and adults for hundreds of years. The narrative ballad, "London Bridge," may have been a rhyme about the actual destruction of London Bridge by King Olaf in the early part of the 11th century. The earliest recorded version ends with the stanza suggesting a man be set to watch the bridge (lines 37–40). The last two stanzas (lines 41–48) are more sophisticated. Have students bring in their old Mother Goose Books or editions from the local library. Compare versions of the rhyme. How many different versions can you locate? (Note: Recent additions to "London Bridges" include stanzas that begin "London Bridge has now been sold," "Arizona's where it is," and "Yankee Doodle keep it up.")

London Bridge is broken down,
Broken down, broken down,
London Bridge is broken down,
My fair lady.   4
Build it up with wood and clay,
Wood and clay, wood and clay,
Build it up with wood and clay,
My fair lady.   8
Wood and clay will wash away,
Wash away, wash away,
Wood and clay will wash away,
My fair lady.   12
Build it up with bricks and mortar,
Bricks and mortar, bricks and mortar,
Build it up with bricks and
mortar,
My fair lady.   16
Bricks and mortar will not stay,
Will not stay, will not stay,
Bricks and mortar will not stay,
My fair lady.   20
Build it up with iron and steel,
Iron and steel, iron and steel,
Build it up with iron and steel,
MY fair lady.   24

Iron and steel will bend and bow,
Bend and bow, bend and bow,
Iron and steel will bend and bow,
My fair lady.   28
Build it up with silver and gold,
Silver and gold, silver and gold,
Build it up with silver and gold,
My fair lady.   32
Silver and gold be stolen away,
Stolen away, stolen away,
Silver and gold be stolen away,
My fair lady.   36
Set a man to watch all night,
Watch all night, watch all night,
Set a man to watch all night,
My fair lady.   40
Suppose the man should fall asleep,
Fall asleep, fall asleep,
Suppose the man should fall asleep,
My fair lady.   44
Give him a pipe to smoke all night,
Smoke all night, smoke all night,
Give him a pipe to smoke all night,
My fair lady.   48

Create a Ballad

A ballad is a song that tells a story in verse. It is one of the oldest forms of poetry and music. During the Middle Ages minstrels wandered throughout Europe performing these types of songs.

There are many ballads that have been preserved from the Middle Ages. Because ballads were sung, rather than written, they often changed. The ballad "Lord Randal" had at least 15 different versions.

Read some ballads. "Lord Randal" (page 34) and "Barbara Allen" (page 35) are excellent examples. More modern ballads include "The Highwayman" by Alfred Noyes, and "Paul Revere's Ride" by Henry Wadsworth Longfellow. "John Henry" is an example of a folk song that is a ballad.

After studying ballads, follow the directions and write your own. Remember a ballad is simply a story where the end word of every other sentence rhymes.

Directions

Step 1

Choose a subject for your ballad. It can be your life, a friend, a sport, or a topic of your choice.

Step 2

The rhyme scheme of a ballad is:

A

B

A

B

Step 3

List pairs of rhyming words.

road, load

course, horse

Step 4

Write sentences about your topic that end with the rhyming words from Step 3.

On a dark and dusty road

He carried his burdensome load

Step 5

Follow the rhyme scheme. Write two stanzas of four lines each.

On a dark and dusty road,	*A*
I chanced to smell a musty horse.	*B*
He carried his burdensome load.	*A*
Along a steady course.	*B*
The smelly horse it did rest,	*C*
While I went into town	*D*
To reach that place I did my best	*C*
So I could soon sit down.	*D*

Step 6

Share it with your classmates.

Questions for Writing and Discussion

Use these questions for both writing and discussion about the novels, *Robin Hood of Sherwood Forest*, *Adam of the Road,* and *The Door in the Wall.* They range from general knowledge to evaluation. The emphasis is to promote creative thought and opinions, allowing the student the opportunity to justify and substantiate his/her opinion with facts from the literary selection and any other resources available to the student.

1. Name all of the characters in the story and what each does.

2. When does the story take place?

3. Where does the story take place?

4. Which character appears first in the story?

5. How does the story end?

6. Retell the story in your own words.

7. How does the main character feel in the story? What are the reasons for his actions?

8. Think of a main event in the story. Why did it happen?

9. Select a picture in the story. Write what happened before and after the picture.

10. Think of a situation that occurred to a person in the story. Decide whether you would have done the same thing or something different. Write what you might have done.

11. If you met Robin Hood and one of his merry men, Adam and Roger, or Robin and John-go-in-the-Wynd, what would you talk about?

12 What part of the story was the funniest? The most exciting? The saddest?

13. Rewrite the story from the point of view of a horse or a deer.

14. Write different endings for the book.

15. Pretend you are a main character in the story. Write a diary about what you are doing each day.

16. Compare two characters in the story. Tell which one you like better and why.

17. Which character in the story would you most like to spend a day with? Why?

18. Was this story worth the time it took to read? Why?

40

Comprehension Techniques

Character Web

A character web is a writing technique which is used to analyze the traits of the main characters in a story. Students should justify their selection of characteristics with examples from the story. This gives a purpose to rereading which improves comprehension.

The name of the character to be analyzed goes in the center circle. The second layer contains the character's traits. Give lots of examples so students don't resort to using adjectives such as "pretty" or "handsome." Some of the character's traits may be found in the handout Characters and their Characteristics (page 42). The third layer gives examples of events from the story to support the trait.

Doing character webs for several characters from the same story allows students to collect data to write comparisons about their characters. They can also personalize the literature by completing a web about themselves and comparing it to one of the book's characters.

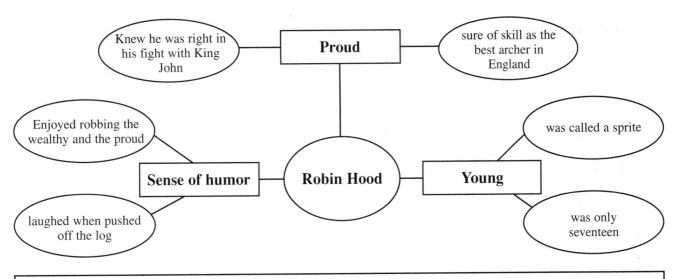

Story Pyramid

This technique is used to look at the main character, story setting, and plot development. At first glance, it appears easy, but it's not. It's a lot like a word puzzle. Students must be precise in their word selection. Have students work in pairs or small groups. Have a dictionary and/or thesaurus available, as well as copies of the text.

Line 1: One word—main character	Robin
Line 2: Two words—describe the main character	Proud Young
Line 3: Three words—setting	Green Sherwood Forest
Line 4: Four words—state the problem	Unjust king rules England
Line 5: Five words—an event	Robin recruits his merry men
Line 6: Six words—an event	Sheriff's archery contest is a trap
Line 7: Seven words—an event	Robin wins the heart of Maid Marian
Line 8: Eight words—solution	Richard returns to England and takes the throne.

Characters and their Characteristics

What is a characteristic ? A characteristic is a special quality or feature that sets one person apart from another.

Listed below are some characteristics. Can you think of characters who fit these descriptions? Which characteristics are possessed by the characters in the story?

Using these characteristics, write a brief description of your favorite medieval character.

humble	brave	courageous	serious
funny	humorous	sad	poor
rich	tall	strong	charming
handsome	pretty	extroverted	selfish
unselfish	self-confident	respectful	considerate
imaginative	inventive	creative	thrilling
independent	intelligent	compassionate	keen
bright	honest	mischievous	friendly
short	adventurous	hard-working	timid
shy	bold	daring	dainty
busy	patriotic	fun-loving	popular
successful	responsible	lazy	dreamer
helpful	happy	disagreeable	simple
fancy	plain	excited	studious
conceited	leader	expert	demanding
gentle	proud	wild	messy
neat	joyful	pitiful	cooperative
loveable	prim	proper	ambitious
able	quiet	curious	reserved
pleasing	bossy	witty	fighter
tireless	energetic	cheerful	smart
good	thoughtful	light-hearted	generous

Journal Writing

Use this journal to record your thoughts after finishing the day's reading.

Name _____

Date _____

My Journal

Today we read _____

_____

_____

_____

_____

_____

_____

_____

_____

_____

_____

_____

_____

_____

_____

_____

Comparison Chart

Use the chart below to compare the ways situations were handled during the Middle Ages to the present. Remember, there may be more than one possible way to deal with each situation.

Situation	Middle Ages	Today
Medical Treatment		
Pest Control		
Telling Time		
Dental Care		
Means of Communication		
Food Production		
Food Storage		
Manufacturing Farm Tools		
Methods of Farming		
Acquiring Clothing		
Means of Travel		
Educational Opportunities		
Forms of Entertainment		

(Think of other problems to compare and write them on the back of this page.)

Dear Diary

Write a diary entry from the point of view of your favorite human or animal character. Be sure to record all of the day's activities and adventures.

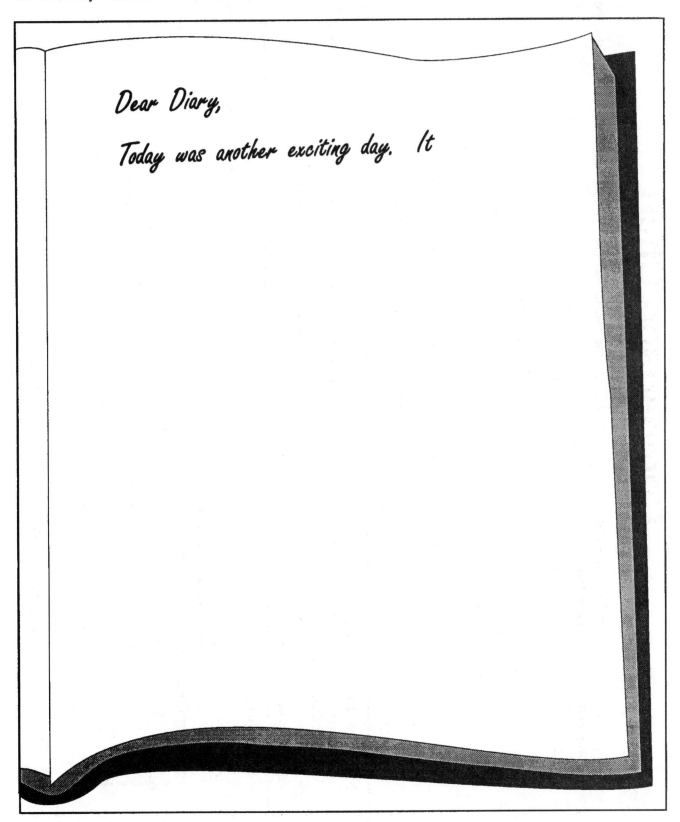

Dear Diary,

Today was another exciting day. It

Medieval Math

The following problem solving activities are based on general information from the unit.

1. In medieval times a cook might make a pie full of little live birds as a surprise for his lord. When the pie was opened, the birds would fly out. In the Mother Goose rhyme "Sing a Song of Sixpence," four and twenty blackbirds were baked in a pie. How many *dozen* birds were there in three pies?

2. In *The Door in the Wall* (page 64), Robin enjoyed a Punch and Judy show. If the Punch and Judy show was performed for 1 score and 8 days and an average of 285 people viewed it each day, how many visitors came to see the show altogether?

3. Daisy chains often served as head ornaments during the Middle Ages. If you made a chain 12 feet 6 inches long and needed to cut 20 inch lengths for each head decoration, about how many could you make?

4. A young noble served as a page at the castle. If he had breakfast from 6:00 A.M. to 6:30 A.M. and then performed daily chores until 7:00 P.M., taking a break for lunch from 1:00 to 1:30 P.M., how many hours did he work at the castle?

5. *Adam of the Road* begins in the year 1294 A.D. How many years ago was this?

6. If during Robin Hood's forty day journey through England he journeyed 300 miles, how many miles of travel did he average each day?

7. A rich nobleman had a feast which consisted of a 12-course meal for each guest. How many courses were served altogether at the feast? (Find the missing fact in this problem, supply one of your own, and solve it.)

8. An archery target has 5 rings, each worth different points: gold=9; red=7; blue=5; black=3; white= 1. If an archer shoots two arrows in the blue ring, one in red, two in gold, and two in black, how many more points will he/she need to score 50 points?

9-12. Use the grid and clues below to fill in the word blanks for exercises 9-12. Then find the coordinates for each letter of the word and write them in the parentheses below. For example, a feline:

C   A   T
(2,3) (1,5) (1,4)

9. the practice, sport, or art of shooting with a bow and arrow

___ ___ ___ ___ ___ ___ ___
(   ) (   ) (   ) (   ) (   ) (   ) (   )

10. wandering performer of poetry and music in the Middle Ages

___ ___ ___ ___ ___ ___ ___ ___
(   ) (   ) (   ) (   ) (   ) (   ) (   ) (   )

11. the main character in *The Door in the Wall*

___ ___ ___ ___ ___
(   ) (   ) (   ) (   ) (   )

12. The red spaniel in *Adam of the Road*

___ ___ ___ ___
(   ) (   ) (   ) (   )

Grid for problems 9–12.

	1	2	3
5	A	M	L
4	T	N	R
3	S	C	B
2	I	O	H
1	K	Y	E

The Art of Butchery

During the Middle Ages, meat and fowl were eaten at banquets. Meat is still a part of many people's diets. Butchers are people who divide meat into various parts. Study the diagram below to see how a steer is butchered today.

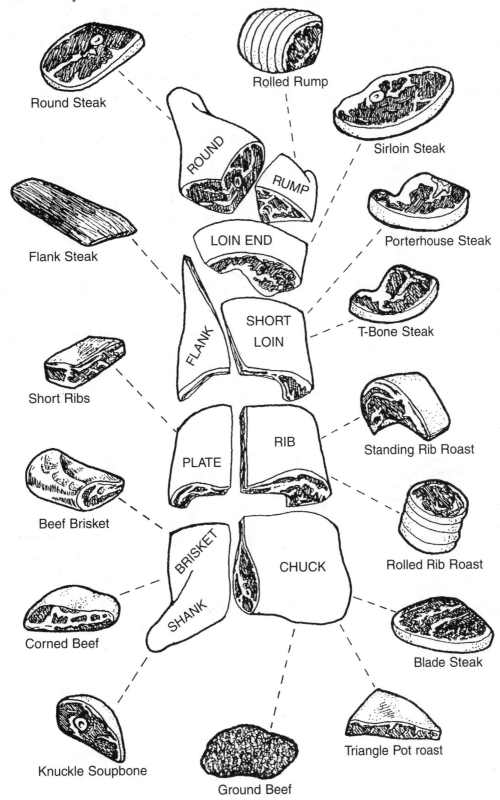

Round Steak

Rolled Rump

Sirloin Steak

ROUND

RUMP

Flank Steak

LOIN END

Porterhouse Steak

FLANK

SHORT LOIN

Short Ribs

T-Bone Steak

Standing Rib Roast

PLATE

RIB

Beef Brisket

Rolled Rib Roast

BRISKET

CHUCK

SHANK

Corned Beef

Blade Steak

Knuckle Soupbone

Ground Beef

Triangle Pot roast

The Art of Butchery *(cont.)*

Using the diagram of the side of beef on page 47, divide the steer into parts, and label each to show what types of meat are cut from each section.

If possible, bring in different types of meat or visit a meat market and compare the textures and colors of the different meat cuts. At a supermarket, check prices and labels of the various beef cuts. Try to find answers to such questions as: Where is the most fat found? Where is the leanest meat found? Why do meat prices change so often? What is the job of a butcher?

Challenge: Bring in recipes for the various cuts of beef.

Very Berry Ink

Before the ballpoint pen, people used a fountain pen that contained ink. Before that, people used a stick or quill pen that had a point and was dipped into the ink. Making and using ink can be a lot of fun. You will need some ripe berries and something for crushing. This was one of the first ways writing ink was produced.

Materials:

ripe blueberries or
strawberries

small jars with lids
(baby food jars
work well)

spoon

paper towels

paper cups

water

eye dropper (optional)

Directions:

1. Remove stems and leaves from ripe berries. Place berries in a small jar. Mixing different kinds of berries will produce different colored inks.

2. Press the berries to a pulp with the back of a spoon.

3. When the berries are crushed, add a little water. Add water by the eye dropper or teaspoon full, one drop at a time. The more water you add, the lighter the color of the ink.

4. Stir the mixture well.

5. Place a sheet of paper towel over a paper cup. Push the paper towel down into the cup.

6. Slowly pour the berry mixture through the towel pressed into the cup.

7. Let all of the liquid drain through the towel. This is the slow part of the process. Remove the towel and throw it away.

8. Pour the strained ink back into the jar. Use the jar as an ink container.

9. Calligraphy pens come in various sizes. A straight pen has a pointed nib and is most like a fountain pen. Experiment with different pen points and shapes. These pens are available at most art and stationery stores.

10. This ink can be used to write letters or copy student-written poems.

The Feudal System

English feudalism is thought to originate in 1066 A.D. In English society, feudalism was characterized by the holding of land from a superior in return for certain services. At the top came the king who claimed ownership of all land and demanded homage from all his senior subjects, barons, bishops, and abbots as his tenants-in-chief. They in turn demanded homage from their knights, and the knights from the freemen and villeins. Each group gave services appropriate to its rank.

Military service consisted of knight service. A tenant was bound to supply his overlord with a fixed number of knights for 40 days a year. If they actually had to fight in a war, they might do so for two months. If there was no war, then they did 40 days of training or garrison duty known as castle-guard. In return, the knight received a fee, land which he looked after, and usually a substantial manor.

Some knights did not fight but performed a serjeantry which might involve carrying the king's banner in battle. Some serjeanties were held lower down on the social scale and involved specific duties, as in the case of Henry de la Wade of Stanton Harcourt who gave fodder for the king's beasts and mowed a hay meadow in Woodstock Park. This may have originated with Henry I's menageries at Woodstock, which reputedly contained lions, leopards, camels, and a porcupine. Sergeanties gradually became obsolete when money became more important in the early thirteenth century. By then military service was being replaced by scutage, or "shield money," and kings could afford paid armies.

The lord's protection was a right which a dutiful vassal could expect to receive. The lord acted as a judge and held a court for his vassals. Freemen could appeal to the King's Court against an unjust lord, but Henry II's itinerant royal judges and trial by jury helped to undermine the noble's power. Eventually villeins could become freemen and burdens at the lowest level of society lessened.

The king maintained special control over some areas. These included the royal manors, royal forests, and towns. Forests were regarded as an important source of sport for the knights and nobles. There were elaborate laws to preserve the beasts in both royal and ordinary forests. Towns had their own courts and customs; the kings had control over them at first but granted them freedom to pursue these customs so that by the late 12th century, towns were increasingly independent.

The Feudal System *(cont.)*

King
The king owned all the land. He made grants of land to his supporters, but in different parts of the country, so that no baron could become too powerful. He kept large areas as royal forests and owned the chief towns and the royal manor.

Land and Protection

Fully-armed Knights

Tenant-In-Chief
Bishops and abbots ranked with barons as tenants-in-chief. They had to provide the king with a certain number of armed knights and their followers had to serve him for 40 days a year. They also had to make various money payments. A tenant-in-chief might be the lord of many manors.

Land and Protection

Knight Service

Sub-Tenant
The country was divided into thousands of "knights' fees", each of which had to provide one fully-armed knight to serve his overlord or the king. Each of these sub-tenants would be the lord of a manor.

Land and Protection

Military and Other Services

Villein
Villeins received land in return for working on the lord's manor at certain times, and making other payments. They could not sell their land.

Serf
Serfs had no land but had to work on the lord's manor at certain times, as well as make other payments.

Scribe, Take a Letter

The life of a serf was filled with little reward and much toil. To help students recognize the role of the serf in the hierarchy of the feudal system, try the following activity.

Background Information

Explain to students that during most of the Middle Ages the only books in existence were manuscripts, since people did not know how to print with type. Therefore, every book had to be painstakingly written by scribes, as the monks who made books were called. Students need to work in pairs for this activity, with one acting as serf and dictating his/her letter to a "monk", using writing process guidelines. Be sure that monk and serf switch roles so that each has an opportunity to write. Final copies are written on parchment prepared by the students. (Tell students that the writing vehicle in medieval times was either vellum, made from calf's skin, or parchment, made from sheep's skin. Parchment was prepared by monks.)

Directions: Imagine that you were a serf and wanted to tell generations to come about your life within the structure of the feudal system. If you could write about a typical day, what would you say? For this activity you will work with a partner who will be your scribe. Since serfs did not write, you will dictate a letter to your partner (a monk), explaining life as a serf, your duties and obligations, and how the feudal system worked. When this activity is completed, you will copy your letters onto prepared parchment.

Materials: Provide the following materials for each student: 9" (23 cm) x 12" (30 cm) white construction paper (at least one per student); 6 oz. or 8 oz. foam cup; tea bag; paper towels (to cover work area), berry ink (page 49) and calligraphy pens (optional)

Preparation: Boil water (enough to supply each student with ½ cup) just before handing out materials. Distribute materials and pour about ½ cup of hot water into foam cups. Direct students to steep tea bag until it is cool enough to handle. Have students tear off about ½" (1 cm) all around the edges of the paper to create a rough edge. Place the construction paper on top of paper towels.

Squeeze tea bag a little and gently rub over construction paper several times. Allow to dry thoroughly. The paper should appear yellowed and aged. If not, apply tea again or make tea stronger. If you opt to use berry ink to copy your letters, check to be sure that it will be clear and dark enough to show up. Otherwise use a more traditional ink. When parchment is ready, students can copy their edited and proofed letters onto it. Complete letters can be presented by having students roll up letters with a ribbon and placing them in a decorated box.

As an alternative, bind letters together into a book. Decorate the cover with pieces from costume jewelry, adding gold and silver ornamentation and a leather-like cover to make it resemble those designed by the monks. These can be displayed at the festival.

Map Sizing

Map sizing is a way to demonstrate how students can enlarge or reduce maps or other pictures. (For practice in using graphs and coordinates, students may enjoy TCM #096 *Challenging Graph Art*.)

Materials: One for each student: map with grid (see below); grid (page 54); pencils

Directions: This activity can be modeled for the class using transparencies made from pages 53 and 54. Reproduce for each student the map on this page and the grid on page 54. Explain to the students that they will be reproducing and enlarging the smaller map. Have them choose vertical and horizontal coordinates (for example B,2) and reproduce and enlarge the configuration in that box on the large grid. As they reproduce the map, they should see a larger map taking shape. As an extension provide various sizes of graph paper, have students plot the coordinates, and enlarge or reduce the map.

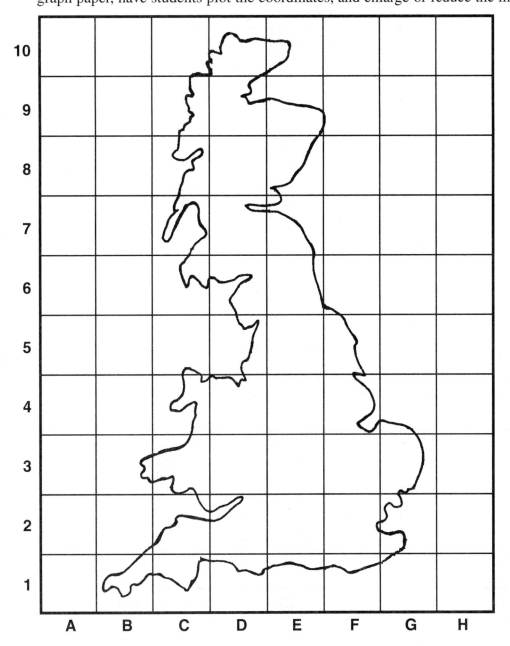

Grid for Map Graphing

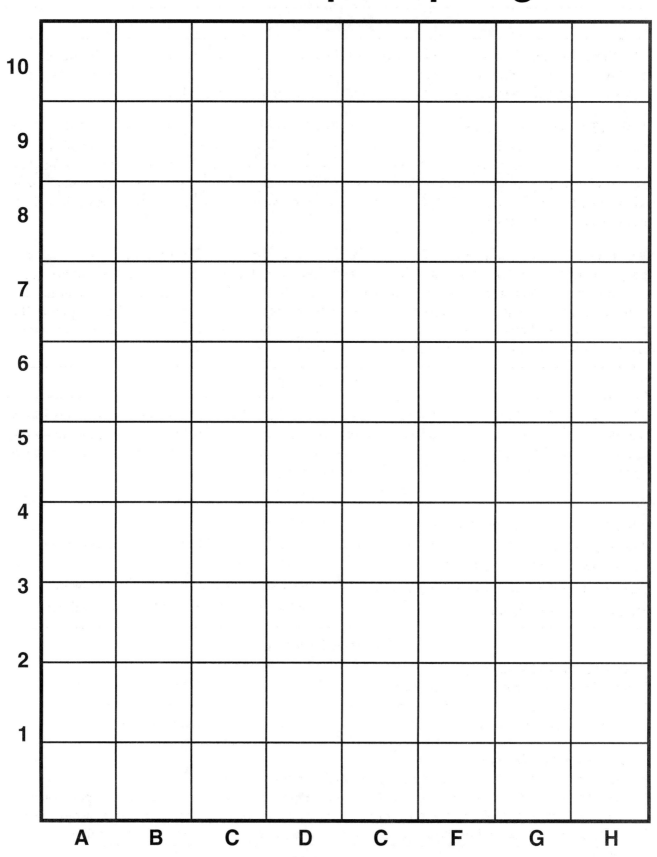

Knights and Armor

Background

The Normans came from France and conquered England in 1066 A.D. after the famous Battle of Hastings. Norman soldiers were famous for their strength and skill in hand-to-hand battle. They wore coats of chain mail (named *hauberks*) and metal helmets with long nose plates.

In the 12th and 13th centuries, many knights went to the Middle East to fight against the Turks. These battles were known as the *Crusades*, and the knights were known as the *Crusaders*. Many of the crusaders were monks as well as soldiers. They wore crosses on their armor and shields, and fought to spread Christianity into the Turkish Empire. The Turkish soldiers, called *Saracens*, were fierce fighters. They wore long robes over their lightweight armor and flowing headdresses. Their style of dress later became popular in Europe.

Knights on horseback were a splendid sight. A knight wore a full suit of metal armor with a crest or badge on his helmet. The armor was very heavy. A knight had to be lifted with pulleys and hoisted onto his horse. The horse was a great animal bred for weight and height. Horses also wore armor to complement the knight's and to protect themselves from being killed, leaving the knight helpless. If a knight fell off his horse, it took several people to help him to his feet. Sometimes a blacksmith would have to hammer a knight's helmet straight so it could be pulled off his head.

Weapons

The weapons of the knights and foot soldiers were designed for hand-to-hand combat. Knights fought one-on-one, facing their enemy, depending upon brute strength to achieve victory. Knights, riding on horseback, did their fighting protected by heavy suits of armor. Foot soldiers used bows and arrows or fought with hand-held weapons. They wore little protection.

Lance: a spear carried by knights on horseback

Longbow and Arrow: used by foot soldiers

Mace: a club made of a ball with spikes attached to a wooden handle, carried by foot soldiers

Dagger: a short-bladed, double-edged knife

Battle Axe: a long-handled axe

Crossbow and Arrow: a compact bow carried by foot soldiers

Sword: a heavy, double-edged steel cutting weapon

Scabbard: a cover or shield for the sword

Halberd: a combination battle-axe and lance

Internet Extenders

The Medieval Paige
http://members.xoom.com/MedPaige/
Activity Summary: This Web site includes links to information about arms and armor, castles, Celtic history, and medieval history. (The download is slow because of many graphics.)

Life in the Middle Ages
http://www.kyrene.k12.az.us/schools/Brisas/sunda/ma/mahome.htm
Activity Summary: Students in a 4th and 5th grade class created this Web site with reports on a variety of topics, including becoming a knight, clothing, jousts and tournaments, and castles. Have students research several of these topics and then create their own illustrated essay on their favorite.

Suit of Armor

In the Middle Ages armor was very expensive. Common soldiers did not wear heavy armor. They wore steel caps and shirts of mail. Knights with horses were the only ones who could afford to wear a full body suit of armor. This armor was so complicated that it took two men to dress a knight. A full body suit was made up of an assortment of steel plates that were attached by hooks and buckles.

Armor was used up to the seventeenth century. As military tactics changed, armor became more of a hindrance then a protection. Helmets and bulletproof vests are the modern version of the armor invented in our early military history.

Boys of noble birth went through many years of training before becoming knights. For seven years or more, a boy lived at the castle as a page, helping the ladies of the castle and training for warfare. Next, he became a squire, or devoted attendant to his lord. The squire, who was preparing for knighthood, polished armor, helped care for the horses, and carried shields and weapons for tournaments and into battle.

Parts of a suit of armor

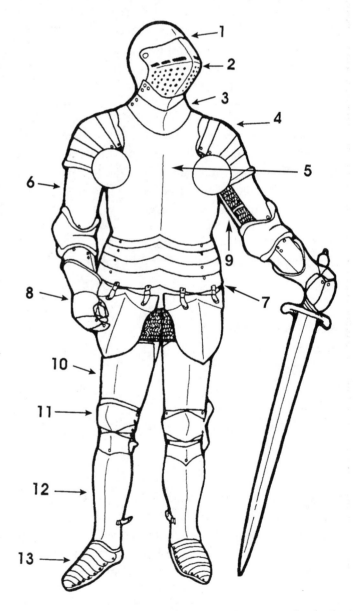

1. **Helmet:** a head covering

2. **Visor:** the moveable part of the helmet in front of the eyes

3. **Gorget:** a collar of metal to protect the throat

4. **Shoulder Piece:** metal that covered the shoulders

5. **Cuirass:** a breast plate from the neck to the waist. The first model of the present day bulletproof vest

6. **Brassard:** armor that protects the arm

7. **Tasset:** overlapping plates that form a short skirt around the hips

8. **Gauntlet:** a glove

9. **Coat of Mail:** Mesh or net made of metal rings or links worn under the armor, chain mail

10. **Cuisse:** a piece of steel that covers the thigh

11. **Elbow Piece:** metal covering the knee and allowing for movement of the leg

12. **Greave:** armor from the ankle to the knee

13. **Sabaton:** armor that covers the foot

A Knight in Armor

Identify the parts and functions of each piece of armor. Using information from page 56, your teacher, or other research materials, label the suit of armor.

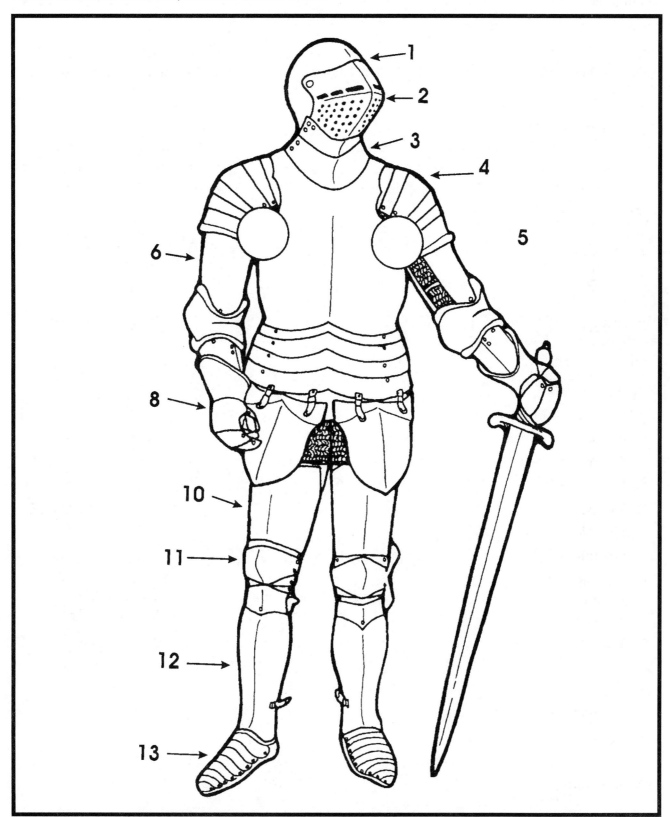

Castles on the Net

Internet Extenders

Life in a Medieval Castle

http://www.castlewales.com/life.html

Activity Summary: Read about the various parts of a castle, including the hall, living quarters, accommodations, kitchen and chapel at this Web site.

Let's Build a Castle

http://score.rims.k12.ca.us/activity/castle_builder/

Activity Summary: Students become medieval castle builders living in Wales in the year 1076. They are hired by the Norman Baron William de Clare to build a fantastic castle in Aberystwyth, Wales. Information is provided to help them design the castle by visiting links to a map of Wales to locate the castle site, life in a medieval castle, glossary of castle terms, other castles, and castle siegecraft and defense. Students are then instructed to draw a blueprint of the castle to scale and, finally, construct a model based on their plans. Scan down this Web page to find a complete lesson plan, including areas to be evaluated and extenders.

Castles on the Web

http://www.castlesontheweb.com/

Summary: This Web site offers links to Castle Greeting cards, abbeys and churches, photo archive, medieval myths and legends, heraldry, and weapons.

The Castles of England

http://members.xoom.com/AndrewMuller/Castles.html

Activity Summary: Click on the map to see photos of castles in various areas of England, Scotland, Wales, and Ireland. There are brief descriptions with each castle.

Ian's Land of Castles

http://www.personal.psu.edu/faculty/n/x/nxd10/castles.htm

Activity Summary: Have students visit this Web site which was created by 10-year old. It uses pictures and brief text to explain various aspects about castles, as well as defenses, beliefs of that time, and castle life. Assign groups of students to create additional information for this Web site.

Off to the Crusades!

Internet Extenders

A Quick Review of the Crusades

http://207.115.207.68/bailey89/crusades/index.htm

Activity Summary: Consider using this Web site to introduce the topic of crusades to the students. If a large screen monitor is available, use it to show the students the four-slide series of the crusades, complete with maps, pictures of the time, and brief descriptions.

The Crusades

http://members.xoom.com/boudica/index.htm

Summary: An excellent history of the crusades can be found here. It is provided through links to the beginning of the crusades and the areas and people involved in them. (Be patient. It takes some time to download this Web site.)

The First Crusade

http://www.brighton73.freeserve.co.uk/firstcrusade/Overview/Overview.htm

Summary: The First Crusade began on November 27, 1095, with a proclamation from Pope Urban II, delivered to clergy and lay folk who had gathered in a field in Clermont, central France. Vivid details of this crusade are provided. Follow the links to learn more about the people and places related to this story.

Map of the First Crusade

http://www.fordham.edu/halsall/maps/1090map.htm

Activity Summary: This Web site is a map showing the areas of Europe and Asia during the time of the First Crusade. Click on highlighted areas to see these enlarged for more detail. Print colored copies of these detailed maps and place them on a bulletin board dedicated to the crusades. Display a modern map of these areas as well and have students compare them to see how they have changed through these centuries.

Map of the Second and Third Crusades

http://www.fordham.edu/halsall/maps/2ndcde.jpg

Activity Summary: A colored map showing the areas involved in the Second and Third Crusades can be found at this Web page. Print a colored copy of this map and add it to the crusades bulletin board.

Tin Can Lanterns

Candleholders were needed to hold the candles people used in their homes, castles, or carried by hand. Lanterns were also hung from the sides of carriages to light the path of the traveler. Tin Can Lanterns make a pretty holder for your newly dipped candles.

Materials:

tin cans washed and cleaned of all paper wrappers and glue, with the bottoms left on; various size nails; tin snips; hammer; string; coat hanger; newspaper or towels; crayons or water-based markers; sand

Directions:

1. Draw a design on the can with crayon or watercolor marker. Do not use a permanent marker. (You do not want the design to show after creating the holes.) Design and work only on one side or area of the can at a time.

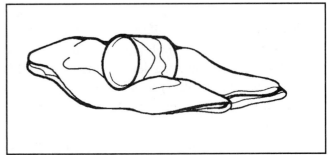

2. Fill can with sand. Put the can on a stack of newspapers or an old towel so it won't roll and to cushion the surface on which you are working.

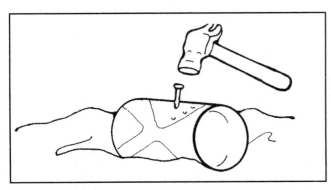

3. Use various nails to create different hole sizes. Hammer holes into the can along the design drawn. Empty sand from can.

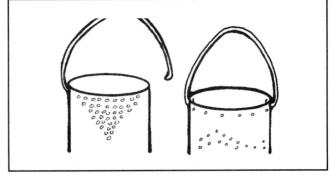

4. Use thin coat hanger wire for handles and hanging loops. Use tin snips to cut hangers. Attach these loops through design holes in the can.

5. Attach candles to the inside of the tin can lantern by melting candle wax to the bottom of the can and placing the candle into the wax while it is still hot. The candle will adhere when the wax cools.

Note: Use extreme caution when working with tin cans as sharp edges on the top and from inside nail holes can cause injuries.

Orange Pomander Ball

The Orange Pomander Ball is an old fashioned closet sweetener. The spicy-smelling ball was used to remove unpleasant odors from the kitchen or cabinets in the house. When the Great Plague swept through Europe in the 14th century, many people tried the pomander as a remedy. However, it did not work.

Materials: whole cloves (one to one and a half boxes per orange); orange; cinnamon (ground); plastic bag; ribbon or netting; string

Directions:

1. Wash and dry the orange well. Make sure there are no breaks or surface bruises on the orange's skin. Push the pointed stems of whole cloves into the skin of the orange very close together until the whole orange is covered with cloves.

2. Sprinkle cinnamon into a plastic bag.

3. Place the orange in the bag.

4. Hold the top of the bag as you shake the orange in the cinnamon.

5. Remove the orange from the bag.

6. Tie a length of ribbon around the orange and knot it. Tie a second ribbon crisscrossing the first ribbon at the bottom and knot it at the top.

7. Tie a length of string around the knotted ribbons.

8. Hang the ball in a special place. The orange will eventually shrink in size and become hard, but should not lose its scent.

9. The top of the orange and bow may be decorated with silk flowers to create an attractive and decorative item.

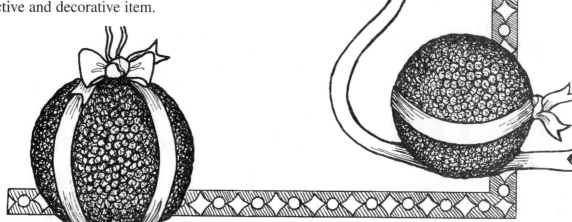

Making a Mural or Banner

Materials:

large pieces of butcher paper; white or brown newsprint; paints (tempera and watercolors); paint brushes of all sizes; sponges, cut in 1/2 inch squares or rectangles to be used like brushes (this gives a very rough effect if paint is dabbed onto the paper); small jars to hold water; felt tip markers; crayons; lots of picture books about the Middle Ages to give ideas for mural

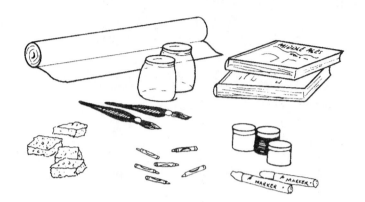

Preparation:

Divide students into small groups. Have them study pictures in books and magazines and choose one to reproduce. Encourage them to try different techniques to get a pleasing effect. Remind them that any mistakes can always be painted over.

Directions:

1. Study pictures of medieval times. Choose one or a portion of one you would like to make into a mural or banner.

2. On a large piece of butcher paper, sketch the chosen picture lightly. The larger the drawing, the easier it will be to paint.

3. After the sketch is completed, paint the background. Crayon may be used to highlight a specific area. The wax will resist the paint and create a pleasing effect.

4. After the background is dry, work toward the front of the picture. Paint the foreground next. When the entire picture is dry add detail. Felt tip markers may be used to highlight specific areas.

5. A 3-D effect can be created by folding construction paper and gluing it to the mural so that it stands away from the background. To get this effect, the mural must be done in stages with the background planned and created first, then the midpoint area, and finally the foreground.

Minstrel's Flute

Materials: Bamboo section about 11½" (29 cm) long by 1" (2.54 cm) in diameter; hand drill; ¼" and ⅜" drill bits; newspaper to cover work surface; ruler; file; skills knife; a cork that fits in the top of the bamboo tube

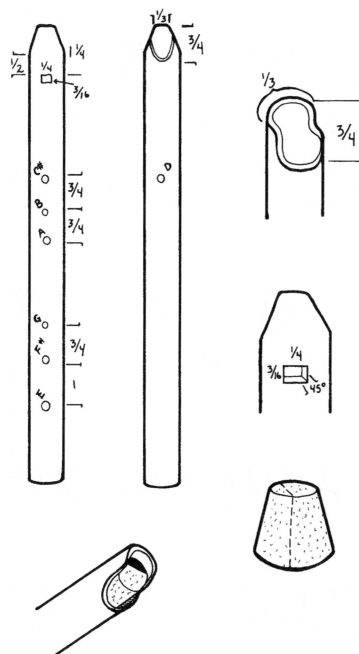

Your flute will have a window and six holes in front and one hole in the back. Measure 1½" (4 cm) from the top opening and cut a small window ¼" (.6 cm) across and 3/16" (.5 cm) down. Measure 2¼" (6 cm) below the window. Drill a ⅜" hole in front (C#) and a smaller hole (¼") in the back, directly behind it (D). Make a ⅜" hole (B) by measuring ¾", (1.8 cm) below C#. Drill a ⅜" hole (A) ¾" below hole (B).

Starting from the bottom of the bamboo section, measure the distance to the window. Divide the result by 4 and drill a ⅜" hole (E) this distance from the bottom of the bamboo section. One inch above the E hole make the F# hole (gouge out a little larger than E). Drill the G hole ¾" above the F# hole. This hole should be smaller than the E hole.

To make the blow hole, measure ⅓" around top front of bamboo section and cut at an angle toward the back so that you finish ¾" below the top opening. Cut the cork on the side so that ⅓" (.8 cm) is sliced away. Use a file to create a channel on the inside of the bamboo shoot where the air will be blown.

Insert the cork to create a small passage for the air.

Optional Activity

The spacings for this flute are the same as an English Recorder. Recorders are easy instruments to learn to play. Schools or school district music departments may have recorders available. Check with students also. Recorder music is available from most music stores. Refer to *The Recorder Book* by Kenneth Wollitz for instructions. A group of students may choose to work together to learn songs which can be played along with the flutes at the festival.

Archery

The bow and arrow were the chief weapons of warfare until the battle of the Spanish Armada in 1588. In that battle firearms became an outstanding success and the bow soon became a secondary war weapon. After the Chinese use of the bow in 1860, it became an obsolete weapon of war.

King Henry VIII was an enthusiastic archer. He institutionalized archery as a sport and insured its success in England as a sport for wagering. Archery is found in almost all societies, from primitive tribes in Africa and South America, to North American Indians, Asian societies, and North European cultures.

Archery equipment consisted of a bow, arrow, a quiver to hold the arrows, and arm guards, or finger protectors.

As part of your Medieval Festival or physical education unit you may wish to try archery with your class.

In Junior Scholastic Archery a round is 24 arrows at 20 and 30 foot ranges.

Scoring is determined in the following way:

- The face of the target has five concentric rings, each bearing a definite scoring value. The center, or gold, scores 9 points for each hit, red scores 7 points, blue scores 5 points, black scores 3 points and white scores 1 point. An arrow that cuts through two colors is given the higher value.

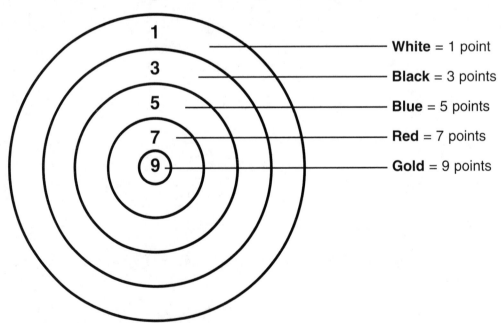

- In creating a target, the radius of the gold ring should be 4.8 inches and the width of all rings should also be 4.8 inches.

- An arrow that has passed through the scoring face, so that it is not visible from the front, counts as 7 points. Rebounding arrows, free from the scoring face shall score 7 points, but they must be witnessed by another person. An arrow embedded in another arrow on the scoring face counts the same as the arrow in which it is embedded.

64

Archery *(cont.)*

- Tie scores are resolved by the greatest number of golds, then reds, then blues, then blacks. Scoring and the drawing of the arrows from the target should be witnessed by all archers shooting on the target.
- A hit made by an archer on a target not assigned to him shall not be counted.

Safety for archery is of the utmost importance. The following rules must be observed.

- Do not wear loose clothing or shirts with pockets which may catch on the bow string.
- Remove all jewelry.
- An arm guard or a finger tab or glove should be worn while shooting to protect your arm.
- Only use equipment which is in good shape. Never shoot with a cracked bow or a split or damaged arrow.

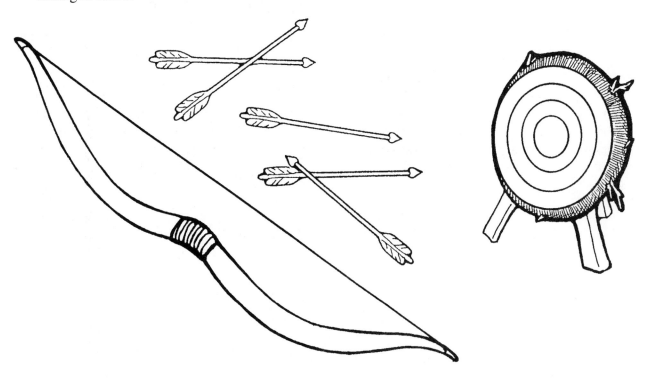

- *Never shoot where or when there is the slightest chance of your arrow hitting anyone.*
- Always shoot at a definite target. Do not shoot aimlessly into the air, or for any great distance unless you are on a range which has a safe flight range.
- *Never use another person as a target, or let a person hold a target for you.*
- All arrows should be shot during the same time period. When all arrows are released, archers should then collect arrows.
- *Never retrieve or cross the shooting line while another archer is shooting. Be sure there is no one behind you before you start removing arrows from the target.*
- Never jerk arrows from the target.
- Archery is a lot of fun, but this fun can quickly turn into a tragedy unless every archer observes common sense safety rules. Accidents don't just happen. They are the result of carelessness or thoughtlessness.

A Medieval Festival

A Medieval Festival is set up like a "Street Faire," which is what it actually is. Along two sides of the playground, blacktop, or quad area, individual areas should be outlined as game booths, craft stalls, and on open-air theater.

1. Tents as game booths are more realistic, but an area roped off for each game or tables set apart will do. Games may include chess, checkers, darts, and a larger area on the grass could be roped off for an archery contest (pages 64 and 65).

2. Tables may be set up to display castles, arts and crafts, and reports completed by the class.

3. A separate area with elaborately decorated chairs could be set up to display the king and queen of the festival. These could be the president and vice president of the student body or a class-elected king and queen for the day. (At some festivals they were the fools of the court.)

4. The stage may be used for the reading of ballads and cinquains to the populace, musical recitals, and short plays (Shakespeare adaptations, Chaucer adaptations, or Biblical plays as seen in *Adam of the Road*).

5. Bulletin board displays from the unit provide additional information and entertainment during the fair. If you choose to have the festival within the classroom, you could invite parents to enjoy a medieval feast and view the activities and projects developed during the unit. Presentation of plays, awards, displays, and musical entertainment will add to the medieval atmosphere.

Preparing a feast for the class can be very simple or very complicated. A simple feast is prepared at home and brought in with the help of parents and aides. A more elaborate affair can be conducted in the class with all the cooking being done by students in the classroom or just outside the room.

To prepare a feast in the room you will need to acquire a crockpot, a barbecue or tabletop broiler, and other electrical cooking aids. Plenty of potholders and wooden cooking utensils should also be kept handy. Have adults supervise any cooking that is in progress. The ideal situation would be to borrow the home economics room for an hour or two after school.

Table settings may be set up on long tables, with a cloth covering, and simple settings. Plates, spoons, and cloth napkins are needed at each place. Other utensils were not used until later in history. Knives were not used on the table.

Peasants sat on each side of the table, and food was displayed in the center. The aristocracy sat along one side of the table, allowing the table to form a U shape. Servants with full platters of food ran up and down the side of the table that was free of chairs, replacing the empty platters.

Internet Extender

Food in Medieval Times

http://www.godecookery.com/godeboke/godeboke.htm

Activity Summary: Read the description of the type of food eaten in medieval times and then visit the next Web site (http://www.godecookery.com/afeast/afeast.htm) to see pictures of medieval feasts shown in six galleries. Print out some of these to display on the bulletin board.

A Medieval Festival *(cont.)*

A suggested menu could include the following:

Wassail	Cheese	Pancakes
Roast fowl or beef	Shortbread	Welsh Rabbit
Yorkshire Pudding	Scones	Bangers

Preparation of fowl or beef:

Meat made up a large part of the 10-to 12-course meals served to nobility. Prepare a favorite recipe to serve at the festival.

If cooking fowl, use these guidelines to help determine your needs:

- 1 chicken (serves 2-4)
- 1 turkey (serves 2-3 per pound of meat)
- 1 cornish hen (serves 1)
- 1 turkey leg (serves 1)

Recipes

Pancakes

Use a pancake mix available at the supermarket or a favorite cookbook recipe. Remember to use caution when cooking with hot oils or fats.

Welsh Rabbit

two slices of white bread

sliced or grated Cheddar cheese

broiler

Preheat the broiler. Toast the slices of bread on one side. Turn them over and toast them very lightly on the other side. When slices are just starting to turn brown, take the broiler pan out and top the bread with a thick layer of sliced or grated cheese. Put the pan back and toast the slices until the cheese is bubbling and half-melted. Be careful not to burn the cheese. Eat while hot. Serves 2.

Yorkshire Pudding (6 servings)

$1/2$ cup all purpose flour

1 teaspoon baking powder

$1/4$ teaspoon salt

pinch of pepper

1 egg

1 cup milk

2 tablespoons lard, vegetable shortening, or beef drippings

In a bowl, sift flour and baking powder. Mix in salt and pepper.

Make a hollow in the center of flour mixture and crack egg into it. Stir well. Add milk grad ually and beat until smooth. Refrigerate at least one half-hour.

One half-hour before the meal is to be served, heat the oven to 425 degrees. Put lard, vegetable shortening, or beef drippings in an 8" (20 cm) x 12" (30 cm) baking pan. Melt lard or shortening. Pour $1/4$ cup cold water into chilled pudding batter and stir well. Then pour mixture into melted lard in the baking pan. Bake 30 minutes. Turn off oven. Let set in closed oven 10 minutes longer. Remove and cut.

A Medieval Festival *(cont.)*

Recipes *(cont.)*

Wassail

(serves 12)

- 2 quarts apple cider
- 2 cups cranberry juice
- $\frac{1}{2}$ cup brown sugar
- 3 sticks cinnamon
- $\frac{1}{2}$ tsp. each ground ginger, allspice
- $\frac{1}{4}$ tsp. ground mace
- 1 large orange, cut into eighths and pierced with whole cloves

Pour all ingredients into a large crockpot. Cover and cook for 1 hour on high, stirring occasionally. Then cook on low for 4 hours.

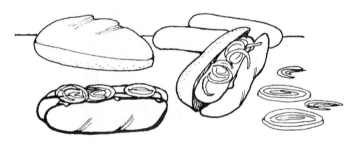

Bangers

Thick rolls (one roll per person)

Polish Sausages or other thick sausages the length of the roll (one per person)

thinly sliced onions ($\frac{1}{2}$ onion per person)

mustard (1 tablespoon per person)

1 tablespoon butter or lard

Saute the onions until golden brown in 1 tablespoon butter.

Set aside and keep warm while you roast or boil the sausage.

Open the rolls to hold the sausage. Coat the rolls with mustard, place a sausage in each roll, and top with onions. Eat hot.

Scones

2 cups all-purpose flour

2 teaspoons baking powder

$\frac{1}{2}$ teaspoon salt

4 tablespoons lard or vegetable shortening

$\frac{1}{4}$ cup sugar

$\frac{1}{4}$ to $\frac{1}{2}$ cup currants or raisins

$\frac{1}{4}$ cup milk or buttermilk

Preheat oven to 425 degrees.

In a large bowl sift flour, baking powder, and salt.

Thoroughly mix in lard with your fingers. Then add the sugar and currants. Mix well.

Stir in enough milk to form a stiff dough.

On a lightly floured surface roll dough out until it is $\frac{3}{4}$ inch (1.8 cm) thick. Cut into 2 inch (5 cm) circles.

Place on a greased, floured cookie sheet and bake in the middle of the oven for about 10 minutes or until the tops are light golden brown. Serve warm with butter and jam or whipped cream.

Makes 12-16 scones.

Research Project

Students can learn more about the Middle Ages by researching the people who influenced it the most. It is important that students realize the role of an historic personality, as it affects current and future events.

Have each student research an important medieval person and present a biographical sketch. Provide reference and other materials for students to use. Set aside one area of the classroom as a project center and/or use a media center for research time. Finished reports can be presented to the class, or posted on a wall or bulletin board.

The biography should place the individual in the context of medieval times and demonstrate how he/she influenced history. For example, after King John lost all lands in the north of France and increased taxation, he fell out of favor with the church and nobility. As a result of increasing hostility, he reluctantly signed the Magna Carta in June of 1215. This document had far-reaching implications and would be an important addition to the biography of King John.

Suggested historical figures to research include:

Eleanor of Aquitaine

King Henry I

Henry II

Thomas Becket

Leif Ericson

Joan of Arc

St. Francis

Richard the Lionhearted

Gutenberg Botticelli

Charlemagne Giotto de Bandone

William the Conqueror

Pope Gregory III

Pope Gregory IX

Boccaccio Chaucer

Dante

St. Bernard

Marco Polo

Fra Angelico

Bulletin Board Ideas

These bulletin boards can easily be assembled by students or the teacher. Student-created bulletin boards reflect the class's interests, needs, and creativity.

Cover the background of the bulletin board with butcher paper, art tissue, construction paper, metallic gift wrap, or cellophane. The background should enhance the display placed on it, rather than detract from it.

Enlarge any of the patterns or clip art (pages 71–72) in this book using an overhead projector or an opaque projector. Attach to background with staples or pins. Pictures, maps, drawings, or actual objects can be used in place of patterns.

A three-dimensional effect can be achieved by layering the objects as you attach them to the board. Cover bulletin area with background. Use $\frac{1}{2}$ inch (1 cm) blocks of cardboard or circles of cardboard cut from a paper towel roll, to make second layer stand away from the background. Blocks will have to be glued to the back of the second layer at key areas, and t-pins used to attach to background.

Label the bulletin board using decorative letters (page 73). Lettering may be enlarged on a copier and pinned onto the board.

Bulletin boards can be used to create interest in the subject or time period, graph the progress of the unit, and aid as a visual stimuli to keep the students on task.

Clip Art

Use this to create bulletin boards, write announcements, or decorate student work.

Internet Extender

Medieval Woodcut Clipart Collection

http://www.godecookery.com/clipart/clart.htm

Activity Summary: This Web site has extensive pictures of medieval woodcuts, including animals, birds, decorative initials, people, and plants. Have students print out some of these to use in creating the bulletin board of Medieval Times.

Clip Art *(cont.)*

72

Decorative Letters

A B C D
E F G H
I J K L
M N O P
Q R S T
U V W X
Y Z

Scroll

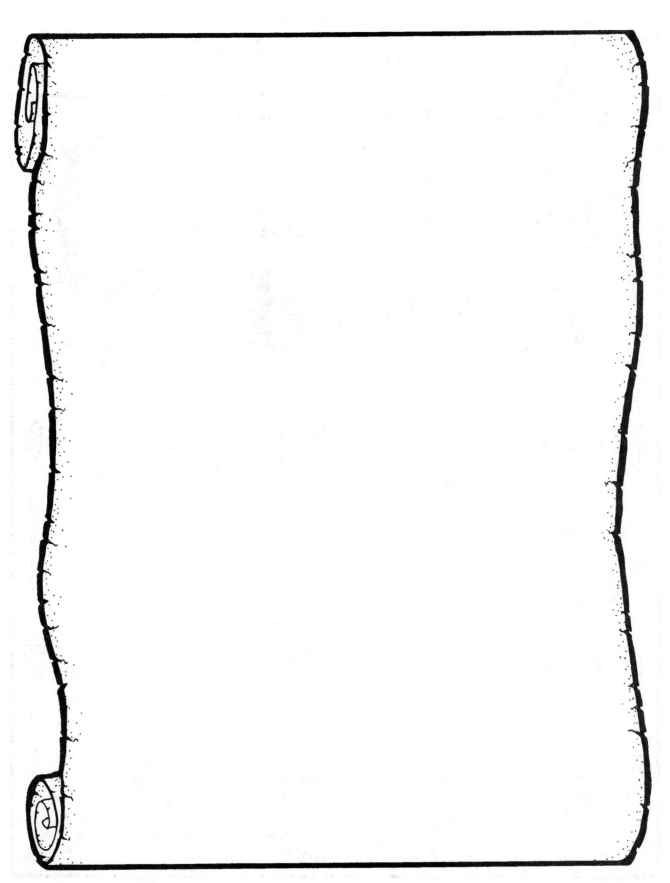

74

Awards

The awards in this section may be reproduced and colored as needed. Awards may be used to show completion of a unit or selection. They are a way to monitor participation and promote on task and completion skills.

Right on Target

Award

Presented to

_____

for

_____

_____

_____   _____
Teacher   Date

Project Award and Invitation

Hear Ye! Hear Ye!

_____ has successfully completed

_____

_____

_____ _____

Teacher   Date

INVITATION

Your presence is requested at a
Medieval Festival in celebration
of our Medieval Times Unit.
Our faire will be held

on _____

at _____

RSVP by _____

Bibliography

Fiction

Carrick, Donald. *Harold and the Giant Knight.* Clarion, 1982)

Ceswick, Paul. *Robin Hood.* (Macmillan, 1984)

Chaucer, Geoffrey. *Canterbury Tales.* (Lothrop, 1988)

DeAngeli, Marguerite. *Book of Nursery and Mother Goose Rhymes.* (Doubleday, 1954)

Delamar, Gloria. *Mother Goose from Nursery to Literature.* (McFarland, 1987)

Glazer, Tom (compiled by). *Tom Glazer's Treasury of Songs for Children.* (Doubleday, 1988)

Green, Roger Lancel. *King Arthur and His Knights of the Round Table.* (Puffin Books, 1984)

Gross, Gwen. *Knights of the Round Table.* (Random House, 1985)

Hunt, Jonathan. *Illuminations.* (Bradbury Press, 1989)

Lobel, Arnold (selected by). T*he Random House Book of Mother Goose.* (Random House, 1986)

Macdonald, Fiona. *A Medieval Castle.* (Bedrick, 1991)

McKinley, Robin. *The Outlaws of Sherwood.* (Greenwillow, 1988)

McSpadden, J. Walker. *The Adventures of Robin Hood and His Merry Outlaws.* (Crown, 1984)

Noyes, Alfred. *The Highwayman.* (Lothrop, 1983)

Scott, Sir Walter. *Ivanhoe.* (Pendulum Press, 1978)

Stevenson, Robert Louis. *The Black Arrow—The Tale of Two Roses.* (Scribner, 1916)

Twain, Mark. *A Connecticut Yankee in King Arthur's Court.* (Harper and Row, 1989)

Westwood, Jennifer. *Medieval Tales.* (Coward-McCann, 1967)

Woods, Ralph L. (ed.) *A Treasury of the Familiar.* (Grolier, 1942, 1964)

Nonfiction

Aliki. *A Medieval Feast.* (Harper, 1983)

Biesty, Stephen. *Stephen Biesty's Incredible Cross-Sections.* (Alfred A. Knopf, 1992)

Black, Irma Simonton. *Castle, Abbey and Town: How People Lived in the Middle Ages.* (Holiday, 1963)

Brooks, Polly Schoyer. *Queen Eleanor.* (Lippincott, 1983)

Buehr, Walter. *Chivalry and the Mailed Knight.* (Putnam, 1963)

Byan, Michele. *Eyewitness Books: Arms & Armor.* (Alfred A. Knopf, 1988)

Caselli, Giovanni. *A Medieval Monk.* (Bedrick, 1986)

Clarke, Richard. *Castles.* (Bookwright, 1989)

Davis, Mary. *Women Who Changed History: Five Famous Queens of Europe.* (Lerner, 1975)

Day, James. *The Black Death.* (Bookwright, 1989)

Denny, Norman and Josephine Filmer-Sankey. *The Bayeux Tapestry: The Story of the Norman Conquest, 1066.* (Atheneum, 1966)

Gravett, Christopher. *Eyewitness Books: Castle.* (Alfred Knopf, 1994)

Hindley, Judy. *The Time Traveler Book of Knights & Castles.* (Usborne Publishing Ltd., 1976)

Howarth, Sarah. *See Through History: The Middle Ages.* (Viking, 1993)

Langley, Andrew. *Eyewitness Books: Medieval Life.* (Alfred A. Knopf, 1996)

Bibliography *(cont.)*

Dugan, Alfred. *Growing up in the Thirteenth Century*. (Pantheon, 1962)

Fremantle, Ann and the Editors of Time-Life Books. *The Age of Faith*. (Time-Life Books, 1965)

Hartman, Gertrude. *Medieval Days and Ways*. (Macmillan Company, 1937)

Hodges, C. Walter. *Magna Carta*. (Coward McCann, 1966)

Hollister, C. Warren, and others. *Medieval Europe: A Sourcebook*. (McGraw-Hill, 1982)

Holme, Bryan. *Medieval Pageant*. (Thames and Hudson, 1987)

Kelly, Amy. *Eleanor of Aquitaine and the Four Kings*. (Harvard University Press, 1950)

Kielty, Bernadine. *The Fall of Constantinople*. (E.M. Hale and Co., 1957)

King, Fred M. *How People Lived in The Middle Ages*. (Benefic Press, 1967)

Macaulay, David. *Castle*. (Houghton Mifflin Co., 1977)

MacDonald, Fiona. *A Medieval Castle*. (Peter Bedrick Books, 1990)

National Geographic Society. *The Age of Chivalry*. (National Geographic Society, 1969)

Oakeshott, R. Ewart. *A Knight and His Horse*. (Dufour Editions, 1964)

A Knight and His Weapons. (Dufour Editions, Philadelphia, 1964)

Osband, Gillian. *Castles*. (Orchard, 1991)

Sancha, Sheila. *The Castle Story*. (Harper and Row, 1979)

Tappan, Eva March. *When Knights Were Bold*. (Houghton Mifflin Company, 1939)

Usborne Cut-Out Models. *Series: Make This Model Village; Cathedral; Town*. (Usborne Publishing Ltd., 1982, 1987)

Williams, Jay. *Knights of the Crusades*. (American Heritage, 1962)

Videos

The Adventures of Robin Hood. (MGM/UA Home Video, 1938)

A Connecticut Yankee in King Arthur's Court. (MCA/Universal Home Video, 1949)

Camelot. (Warner Home Video, 1967)

The Court Jester. (Paramount Home Video, 1956)

Henry V. (Paramount Home Video, 1944; CBS/Fox Video, 1990)

Ivanhoe. (MGM/Universal Home Video, 1952)

Knights of the Round Table. (MGM/UA Home Video, 1953)

London and Surrounding Day Trips. (Republic Pictures Home Video, 1956)

The Prince and the Pauper. (MGM/UA Home Video, 1937)

The Princess Bride. (Cary Elwes Nelson Entertainment, 1987)

Richard III. (Nelson Entertainment Release, 1955)

Robin Hood. (Walt Disney Productions)

The Sword in the Stone. (Walt Disney Production)

Answer Key *(cont.)*

Sequencing and Summary (page 11)

Unscramble Paragraph: *Robin Hood of Sherwood Forest*—chapter 1

First Robin competed with a forester in an archery contest.

Later Robin is charged with the crime of killing a king's deer.

Then Robin escapes into the forest.

Next He swears to fight unjust laws.

Finally He forms a band of outlaws.

Fill in the blanks: *Robin Hood of Sherwood Forest*—chapter 2

Answers will vary. Accept any word order that shows a progression of order or sequencing.

Mathematics in Sherwood Forest (pages 12–13)

1. a. $12 + 21 + 12 = 45$ feet
   b. $45 \times 1/5 = 9$ feet

2. a. $54" + 18" = 72" = 6$ feet

3. a. $\$5 \times 10 = \$50$
   b. $6 \times 10 = 60$ gold pieces

4. a. $20 \times 5 = 100$ men
   b. $1209 - 1176 = 33$ years
   (rounds off to 2 score)

5. $7 - 1 = 6$ feet tall

6. a. $42 \div 7 = 6$ weeks b. $42 \div 7 = $ 6th day

7. a. $2 \times 20 = 40$ b. $40 + (3 \times 20 + 7) = 107$ men

Crossword (page21)

Word Search (page 30)

A grid puzzle with words including: MOTHER, DEVOTION, SHEEP, CAT, WESTMINSTER, WINDHOLE, PATIENCE, FOG, LUKE, SIR, THE DOOR IN THE WALL, URCHIN, CRUTCH, JOUSTING, PATIENCE, FISHMONGER, PARCHMENT, LUNCH

Comprehension Questions (page 36)
"Lord Randal"

1. Lord Randal and his mother.

2. She calls him "her son," and Randal calls her mother.

3. Randal is ill and presumed poisoned by his girlfriend.

4. He likes to hunt; he's ill and tired; he feels in love; he's young and handsome; he's the eldest son with a sister and a brother; he's rich and has lots of property. (answers will vary)

5. She's possessive and jealous; she nags; she's greedy; she dislikes his sweetheart; she's panicked by his sudden illness. (answers will vary)

6. When she hears that the hawks and hounds are dead.

7. He's making out a verbal will, dividing and leaving all he owns to his family.

8. His sweetheart.

9. In the Greenwood.

10. Poison and fire.

11. Answers will vary.

12. Answers will vary: Lie down and rest and be left alone or make out his will and set his affairs in order before he dies.

Answer Key (cont.)

"Barbara Allen" (page 36)

1. Barbara Allen, Jemmy Grove, Jemmy Grove's manservant.

2. In the month of May: Spring.

3. Jemmy Grove.

4. He has been sent to ask Barbara Allen to come to his dying master.

5. She is a very proud person, who holds a grudge and hides her feelings.

6. A servant has been sent to fetch Barbara Allen to come to his dying master's side. Barbara Allen does not appear to be in a hurry to go to the young man, or care about his demise.

7. Answer may vary. They should include some mention of her coldness to the young man and her reprimand to him for slighting her.

8. Jemmy Grove dies.

9. Answers may vary.

10. She begins to feel the loss and have feelings of guilt and regret.

11. The fault of pride.

12. Answers may vary.

"Barbara Allen" and "Lord Randal" Comparison (page 37)

1. a. ABAB construction; 40 lines, 10 stanzas of 4 lines each.

   b. Barbara Allen: second and fourth line in each stanza have an obvious rhyme. First and third lines do not rhyme. Lord Randal: First and third line of each stanza rhyme. First line of each stanza ends with son. Second line of each stanza ends with man. Third line of each stanza ends with soon. Fourth line of each stanza ends with down.

2. a. Both have a young man dying for unrequited love. Both are talking to their mothers. Both main characters die because they love the wrong person.

   b. They are of different classes and sexes. Lord Randal dies as a direct result of his loving the wrong person. Barbara Allen dies as an indirect result of loving the wrong person.

3. Barbara Allen: proud, vengeful, sensitive, easily offended, hiding her true feelings. Lord Randal: sensitive, trusting, henpecked by mother.

4. Unrequited love.

5. Answers will vary.

6. Answers will vary.

7. Answers will vary.

8. They both have to deal with dramatic results in the lives of people who are driven by emotion and a romantic view and expectation of life and loving.

9. Results will vary.

10. Results will vary.

11. Results will vary.

Medieval Math (page 46)

1. $(20 + 4) \times 3 = 72 \div 12 = 6$ dozen

2. $(20 + 8) \times 285 = 7980$ people

3. $(12 \times 12) + 6 \div 20 = 7\frac{1}{2}$ (round to 7 chains)

4. 6:00 a.m. to 7:00 p.m.= 13 hrs. – 1 hr. = 12 hrs.

5. Current year: 1294

6. $300 \div 40 = 7\frac{1}{2}$ miles per day

7. missing fact = How many guests were at the feast? Answers will vary.

8. $50 - (5 + 5 + 7 + 9 + 9 + 3 + 3) = 9$ points

9. archery (1,5) (3,4) (2,3) (3,2) (3,1) (3,4) (2,1)

10. minstrel (2,5) (1,2) (2,4) (1,3) (1,4) (3,4) (3,1) (3,5)

11. Robin (3,4) (2,2) (3,3) (1,2) (2,4)

12. Nick (2,4) (1,2) (2,3) (1,1)